POETIC
JUSTICE

THE ALEXANDER ROSENTHAL LECTURES
NORTHWESTERN UNIVERSITY LAW SCHOOL

POETIC JUSTICE

The Literary Imagination and Public Life

Martha C. Nussbaum

BEACON PRESS

BOSTON

Beacon Press
25 Beacon Street
Boston, Massachusetts 02108-2892

Beacon Press books
are published under the auspices of
the Unitarian Universalist Association of Congregations.

99 98 97 96 95   8 7 6 5 4 3 2 1

Text design by Elizabeth Elsas

Library of Congress Cataloging-in-Publication Data

Nussbaum, Martha Craven, 1947–
    Poetic justice : the literary imagination and public life / Martha
C. Nussbaum.
        p. cm.
    Includes bibliographical references and index.
    ISBN 0-8070-4108-4
    1. Politics and literature.   2. Literature and society.
3. Literature—Social aspects.   I. Title.
PN51.N78   1995
809'.93358—dc20   95-18076

TO RICHARD POSNER

A child said *What is the grass?* fetching it to me with full hands,
How could I answer the child? I do not know what it is any more than he.

I guess it must be the flag of my disposition, out of hopeful green stuff woven.

Or I guess it is the handkerchief of the Lord,
A scented gift and remembrancer designedly dropt,
Bearing the owner's name someway in the corners, that we may see and remark,
   and say *Whose?*

Or I guess the grass is itself a child, the produced babe of the vegetation.
Or I guess it is a uniform hieroglyphic;
And it means, Sprouting alike in broad zones and narrow zones,
Growing among black folks as among white,
Kanuck, Tuckahoe, Congressman, Cuff, I give them the same, I receive them the
   same.

And now it seems to me the beautiful uncut hair of graves.

Tenderly will I use you curling grass,
It may be you transpire from the breasts of young men,
   It may be that if I had known them I would have loved them,
It may be you are from old people, or from offspring taken soon out of their
   mother's laps,
And here you are the mother's laps.

This grass is very dark to be from the white heads of old mothers,
Darker than the colorless beards of old men,
Dark to come from under the faint red roofs of mouths.

Walt Whitman, Song of Myself

For the first time in his life he had gained a pinnacle of feeling upon which he
could stand and see vague relations that he had neer dreamed of. If that white
looming mountain of hate were not a mountain at all, but people, people like
himself, and like Jan—then he was faced with a high hope the like of which he
had never thought could be, and a despair the full depths of which he knew he
could not stand to feel.

Richard Wright, Native Son

[Contents]

[Acknowledgments]

This book began as the Alexander Rosenthal Lectures for 1991 at the Northwestern University Law School. Portions were also presented as Hanna Lectures at Hamline University, as the Arthur Leff Fellow's lectures at the Yale University Law School, and as Donnelan Lectures at Trinity College, Dublin. My first thanks are therefore owed to my hosts at these institutions, for their hospitality and their extremely valuable comments— and especially to Akhil Amar, Ron Allen, Owen Fiss, Paul Gewirtz, Anthony Kronman, and Bill Lyons. During the evolution of the manuscript I have received comments from many people on many drafts. I cannot do justice to them all, but at least I want to thank Brian Bix, Dan Brock, Ken Dornstein, Elliott Dunn, Don Garrett, David Gorman, Tom Grey, Jean Hampton, Linda Hirshman, Sanford Kadish, Michael McConnell, Philip Quinn, Eric Rasmusen, Henry Richardson, Amartya Sen, Cass Sunstein, Jeremy Waldron, James Boyd White, and Bernard Williams. I am also particularly grateful to the students in my Law and Literature course at the University of Chicago Law School in 1994.

One debt is of special importance. The night before I gave my first Rosenthal Lecture, I had the good fortune to be introduced to the person who was in many ways that lecture's Mr. Gradgrind; and my intellectual adversary throughout the series. I was told that he had been given the text of my lectures. I approached the dinner with some apprehensiveness, knowing how common it is to resent criticism and to disdain the critic. My fears were soon allayed, however, since I encountered a person of tremendous joie de vivre and openness, whose appetite for the exchange of argument is indefatigable, especially where there is deep disagreement. I also found him to be a lover of novels and a most literary judge, so that our disagreement proved a far more subtle one than I had expected. It has, I hope, over time, made my own arguments more subtle as well. For his generosity in arguing with me for years (and I trust he won't stop now), his tireless energy in producing comments, and his great capacity for friendship, I dedicate this book with affection to Richard Posner.

[Preface]

Speaking of political argument in America, Walt Whitman wrote that the literary artist is a much-needed participant. The poet is "the arbiter of the diverse," "the equalizer of his age and land." His capacious imagination "sees eternity in men and women" and "does not see men and women as dreams or dots." Whitman's call for public poetry is, I believe, as pertinent to our time as it was to his. Very often in today's political life we lack the capacity to see one another as fully human, as more than "dreams or dots." Often, too, those refusals of sympathy are aided and abetted by an excessive reliance on technical ways of modeling human behavior, especially those that derive from economic utilitarianism. These models can be very valuable in their place, but they frequently prove incomplete as a guide to political relations among citizens. Without the participation of the literary imagination, said Whitman, "things are grotesque, eccentric, fail of their full returns." We see much political argument today that is grotesque and eccentric in this way. The purpose of this book is to describe the ingredient of public discourse that Whitman found missing from his America and to show some roles it still might play in our own. It grows out of the conviction, which I share with Whitman, that storytelling and literary imagining are not opposed to rational argument, but can provide essential ingredients in a rational argument.

During the lifetimes of William James and John Dewey, it was taken for granted that academic philosophy, including philosophical discussion of literature and art, was part of public discourse. But during much of the present century, academic philosophy in the United States has had relatively few links with practical choice and public life.[1] Recently, however, philosophers have once again become involved in public debate, not only about the basic issues of ethical and political theory, but also about more concrete issues in medicine, business, and law. During the past five years I, like numerous philosophical colleagues, have spent more and more time in professional schools—law schools in my case—giving visiting lectures and talking about issues with professional theorists and practitioners. In the spring of 1994, I taught law students for the first time, as a visiting professor in the law school at the University of Chicago. The present book owes a great deal to these experiences.

The subject of my legal teaching was, in fact, storytelling, for the course I was asked to teach was Law and Literature. The law students and I read Sophocles, and Plato, and Seneca, and Dickens. In connection with the literary works, we discussed compassion and mercy, the role of the emotions in public judgment, what is involved in imagining the situation of someone different from oneself. We talked about ways in which texts of different types present human beings—seeing them, in some cases, as ends in themselves, endowed with dignity and individuality, in others as abstract undistinguishable units or as mere means to the ends of others. Since the University of Chicago Law School is the birthplace of the law-and-economics movement, we discussed the relationship between the literary imagination and economic reasoning.

We talked, as well, about more concrete social issues, including gender, homosexuality, and race. In a lecture hall less than fifty yards away from the black metal fence in the law school parking lot that marks the "line" between the world of the university and the world of the inner-city Chicago slums, in a class with only one African-American member in seventy, we read Richard Wright's *Native Son*. Every Chicago place name marked a location we knew—though with respect to some of those locations almost all of us were in the position of Wright's Mary Dalton, when she says to Bigger Thomas that she has no idea how people live ten blocks away from her. "He knew as he stood there," says Wright of Bigger, "that he could never tell why he had killed. It was not that he did not really want to tell, but the telling of it would have involved an explanation of his entire life." We talked about the relevance of that passage to disputes about discretion and mercy in criminal sentencing—about a Supreme Court decision that instructs courts to treat defendants not "as members of a faceless, undifferentiated mass" but "as uniquely individual human beings."[2] What might the role of a novel such as Wright's be, in conveying to future judges and lawyers an understanding of that requirement? I did not invent the course Law and Literature; in fact, it had been for some years a regular part of the law school's curriculum.[3] The legal profession's interest in the relationship between philosophy and literature had at first surprised me. Gradually I had come to see that what was being sought from such teaching was the investigation and principled defense of a humanistic and multivalued conception of public rationality that is powerfully exemplified in the common-law tradition. This conception needs defending, since it has for some time been under attack from the more "scientific" conceptions offered by the law-and-economics movement. I had for some time been working on related philosophical ideas and had already begun to connect them to issues in the law. But the Chicago course marked the first time that I had tried to work out some of these ideas in the classroom, interacting with students who would shortly be lawyers and clerks for judges. Although I remain a legal amateur, and although I make this suggestion from the outside, still in considerable ignorance of the more technical and formal side of the law, which I am not proposing to demote and for which I have great respect, I believe more strongly than ever that thinking about narrative literature does have the potential to make a contribution to the law in particular, to public reasoning generally.

During this period, I also became involved in public life in a completely different area. From 1986 to 1993 I was a consultant at the World Institute for Development Economics Research in Helsinki (a research institute connected with the United Nations) as codirector, with economist Amartya Sen, of a project on quality of life assessment in developing countries. Our project was to show how debates in philosophy—about cultural relativism and antirelativism, about utilitarianism and its strengths and weaknesses—were relevant to the work of policy makers as they attempt to find ways of measuring and comparing that elusive thing, "the quality of life" in a nation. Here, too, narrative literature played an important part. In fact, Sen and I used Dickens's *Hard Times* to develop criticisms of standard economic paradigms of quality of life assessment, which seemed to us reductive and lacking in human complexity, and to illustrate the types of information such assessments would need to include in order to be fully rational, offering good guidance of both a predictive and a normative type.[4] Once again, the ability to imagine the concrete ways in which people different from oneself grapple with disadvantage seemed to us to have great practical and public value. We argued that a complete economic science needs to work with an expanded conception of the quality of life if its indispensable technical investigations are to be fully successful. (I discuss those arguments in chapter 2.)

The literary imagination is a part of public rationality, and not the whole. I believe that it would be extremely dangerous to suggest substituting empathetic imagining for rule-governed moral reasoning, and I am not making that suggestion. In fact, I defend the literary imagination precisely because it seems to me an essential ingredient of an ethical stance that asks us to concern ourselves with the good of other people whose lives are distant from our own. Such an ethical stance will have a large place for rules and formal decision procedures, including procedures inspired by economics. (My own preferred version of the ethical stance derives from Aristotle, but everything I say here could be accommodated by a Kantianism modified so as to give the emotions a carefully demarcated cognitive role.)[5] On the other hand, an ethics of impartial respect for human dignity will fail to engage real human beings unless they are made capable of entering imaginatively into the lives of distant others and to have emotions related to that participation. The emotions of the reader or spectator have been defended as essential to good ethical judgment by quite a few ethical theorists deeply concerned about impartiality—perhaps most notably by Adam Smith, whose *Theory of Moral Sentiments* is a central inspiration for the project of this book. Although these emotions have limitations and dangers, as I shall argue, and although their function in ethical reasoning must be carefully circumscribed, they also contain a powerful, if partial, vision of social justice and provide powerful motives for just conduct.

But will it do any good to appeal even to the best uses of the literary imagination in a political climate filled with prejudice and hatred? For Big-

ger Thomas, the realization that white people each had individual stories to
tell brought the hope of human solidarity. But it also brought despair, born
of the knowledge that hatred and obtuseness were politically more powerful
than hope, that only one rare person had been able to see him in the light
of that hope, and that, for him at any rate, all hope would shortly be extin-
guished with his life. Does it do any good to tell stories, then, in a world in
which many people's daily lives are dominated by various forms of exclusion
and oppression? (And where stories themselves can play a role in that oppression?) In the final examination of my Law and Literature course, one of
my students, critical of my optimistic view of the role of literature, wrote the
following words about our classroom reading of E. M. Forster—anony-
mously, since exams in Chicago are graded by number only:

> Possibly reading a work such as *Maurice* would change an individual's mind,
> perhaps a judge's mind. I fear however in most cases it would not. Perhaps
> many such works could force someone who abhors homosexuality to exam-
> ine his or her reasons for doing so. But it seems like such a tiny bulwark of
> hope against a storm of prejudice and hatred.

Student 1180 is correct.[6] The literary imagination has to contend against
the deep prejudices of many human beings and institutions and will not
always prevail. Many people who tell wonderful stories are racists who could
not tell an individualized empathetic story about a black person. Many
people who have great sympathy in matters of race refuse Forster's invitation
to imagine a gay person as someone they or one of their loved ones might
be. Our society is full of refusals to imagine one another with empathy and
compassion, refusals from which none of us is free. Many of the stories we
tell one another encourage the refusal of compassion, so not even the literary imagination itself is free from blame. Even when we have found a good
story to tell, we should not hope to change years of institutionalized abhor-
rence and discrimination by appeal to "fancy" alone, since fancy, even when
adequately realized, is a fragile force in a world filled with various forms of
hardness. We have reason to sympathize with this student's critique when
we consider the way some of these issues are treated in practical politics,
which frequently does seem impervious both to argument and to compassion, refusing the claim of another person's story.

On the other hand, what we see in such human refusals is not a defect in the type of "fancy" I shall be defending here, but a defect in human beings who do not exercise that type of fancy well, who cultivate their human sympathies unequally and narrowly. The remedy for that defect seems to be, not the repudiation of fancy, but its more consistent and humane cultivation; not the substitution of impersonal institutional structures for the imagination, but the construction of institutions, and institutional actors, who more perfectly embody, and by institutional firmness protect, the insights of the compassionate imagination. We need not and should not rely on the fancy of individuals alone. Institutions themselves should also be informed by "fancy's" insight.

So I want to say to Student 1180, What else can we do as citizens, if we want to have hope and to respect ourselves? The task of the literary imagination in public life is, as Henry James once put it, to "*create* the record, in default of any better enjoyment of it: to imagine, in a word, the honourable, the producible case."[7] We may hope that this record will stand, even when it does not universally persuade, and that by standing next to crudeness and obtuseness as a fine thing next to an ugly thing, it will testify to the value of humanity as an end in itself. If we do not cultivate the imagination in this way, we lose, I believe, an essential bridge to social justice. If we give up on "fancy," we give up on ourselves.

This book lies at the intersection of several more technical philosophical projects in which I am currently engaged. It will allude to, though not fully develop, the work on establishing a framework for quality of life assessment. It will allude to evolving work on legal rationality and the role of the emotions and imagination in the law. And finally—focusing on connections between the literary imagination and both compassion and mercy—it will allude to a much more detailed work in progress on the structure of the emotions themselves and the role of belief and thought in emotions. The aim of this book is not to pursue any of these projects exhaustively. It is, instead, to present a vivid conception of public reasoning that is humanistic and not pseudo-scientific, to show how a certain type of narrative literature expresses and develops such a conception, and to show some of the benefits this conception might have to offer in the public sphere. Justice Oliver Wendell Holmes once wrote that a study of Aristotle can show us that "life is painting a picture not doing a sum."[8] The purpose of this book is to elaborate that idea and to show what public reasoning in that spirit might look like.

POETIC
JUSTICE

1

The Literary Imagination

Noting in his children a strange and unsavory exuberance of imagination, an unwholesome flowering of sentiment—in short, a lapse from that perfect scientific rationality on which both private and public life, when well managed, depend—Mr. Gradgrind, economist, public man, and educator, inquires into the cause:

> "Whether," said Mr. Gradgrind, pondering with his hands in his pockets, and his cavernous eyes on the fire, "whether any instructor or servant can have suggested anything? Whether Louisa or Thomas can have been reading anything? Whether, in spite of all precautions, any idle story-book can have got into the house? Because, in minds that have been practically formed by rule and line, from the cradle upwards, this is so curious, so incomprehensible."[1]

Mr. Gradgrind knows that storybooks are not simply decorative, not simply amusing—though this already would be enough to cause him to doubt their utility. Literature, he sees, is subversive. It is the enemy of political economy, as Mr. Gradgrind knows it: an all-encompassing scientific project committed to representing the complexities of human life in "tabular form." Literature expresses, in its structures and its ways of speaking, a sense of life that is incompatible with the vision of the world embodied in the texts of political economy; and engagement with it forms the imagination and the desires in a manner that subverts that science's norm of rationality. It is with good reason, from his point of view, that Mr. Gradgrind teaches Sissy Jupe, the uneducated circus girl, to regard the storybooks she once lovingly read to her father as "wrong books," about which the less said the better. And it is with good reason that he lapses into depression about the nation's future when he considers the citizens who, flocking to the public libraries of Coketown, "took DeFoe to their bosoms, instead of Euclid, and seemed to be on the whole more comforted by Goldsmith than by Cocker." When idle storybooks get into the house, political economy is at risk. The world is seen in a new way, and uneconomical activities of fancying and feeling are both represented and, worse still, enacted.

Mr. Gradgrind is right: literature and the literary imagination are subversive. We are accustomed by now to think of literature as optional: as great, valuable, entertaining, excellent, but something that exists off to one side of political and economic and legal thought, in another university department, ancillary rather than competitive. The segmentation of the modern academy—along with narrowly hedonist theories of literary value—has caused us to lose hold of the insight that Mr. Gradgrind securely grasped: that the novel (for from now on I shall focus on novels) is a morally controversial form, expressing in its very shape and style, in its modes of interaction with its readers, a normative sense of life.[2] It tells its readers to notice this and not this, to be active in these and not those ways. It leads them into certain postures of the mind and heart and not others. And as Mr. Gradgrind all too clearly perceived, these are the wrong ways, and highly dangerous postures, from the point of view of the narrow conception of economic rationality that is, in his view, normative for both public and private thought.

But if literature is, from the Gradgrind economist's viewpoint, dangerous and deserving of suppression, this implies as well that it is no mere frill, that it has the potential to make a distinctive contribution to our public life. And if one should have some doubts about the books Mr. Gradgrind favors—as to their adequacy as visions of humanity, expressions of a complete sense of social life—one might then see in the very zeal of Mr. Gradgrind's repudiation a reason to invite idle storybooks into the house to plead their cause. And if they should plead their cause successfully, we might have compelling reasons to invite them to stay: not only in our homes and schools, shaping the perceptions of our children, but also in our schools of public policy and development studies, and in our government offices and courts, and even in our law schools—wherever the public imagination is shaped and nourished—as essential parts of an education for public rationality.

I shall focus, then, on the characteristics of the literary imagination as a public imagination, an imagination that will steer judges in their judging, legislators in their legislating, policy makers in measuring the quality of life of people near and far. Commending it in the public sphere is difficult, since many people who think of literature as illuminating about the workings of the personal life and the private imagination believe that it is idle and unhelpful when the larger concerns of classes and nations are at issue. Here, it is felt, we need something more reliably scientific, more detached, more sternly rational. But I shall argue that here, all the more, literary forms have a unique contribution to make. I shall make this case by focusing on the novel, to begin with, on Dickens's *Hard Times,* which takes as its explicit theme the contribution of the novel to moral and political life, both representing and enacting the novel's triumph over other ways of imagining the world. Both in this chapter and throughout my argument, I shall discuss the reasons for this choice and its implications for any general conclusions about "the literary imagination." "Political economy" is also a large category, including economic thinkers of many types. The antagonist throughout will be, not sophisticated philosophical forms of utilitarianism, and also not the economics of the most distinguished philosophical economists, such as Adam Smith in the eighteenth century and Amartya Sen in this one, but cruder forms of economic utilitarianism and cost-benefit analysis that are actually used in many areas of public policy-making and are frequently commended as normative for others. In fact, my proposals will draw on the insights of both Smith and Sen to propose a more expansive conception of "political economy." I shall focus on two practical questions, connected with the two areas of my own experience in public life: the question, first, of measuring the well-being of a population, and second, the nature of the rational processes of the good judge or legal thinker. The first is explicitly a central topic of *Hard Times;* the second is an implicit theme that the novel as a whole powerfully develops. Both are good places to see the contrast between the economic and the literary at work. I shall be asking what activities of the personality are best for these two public tasks, what thoughts, what sentiments, what ways of perceiving. This will lead us naturally to ask which texts represent these desired activities and call them into being.

My question, then, will be not just about what novels represent, what goes on inside them, although that is an important part of my project. But I also want to ask what sense of life their forms themselves embody: not only how the characters feel and imagine, but what sort of feeling and imagining is enacted in the telling of the story itself, in the shape and texture of the sentences, the pattern of the narrative, the sense of life that animates the text as a whole. And I shall ask as well, and inevitably, what sort of feeling and imagining is called into being by the shape of the text as it addresses its imagined reader, what sort of readerly activity is built into the form.

The contest between the literary imagination and its rivals can best be focused by starting from three objections commonly made against "fancy" when public policy-making is in question. Mr. Gradgrind knew those objections well. First, it will be said that the literary imagination is unscientific and subversive of scientific social thought. Second, it will be said that it is irrational in its commitment to the emotions. Third, it will be charged that it has nothing to do with the impartiality and universality that we associate with law and public judgment. I shall devote one chapter to each of these objections. Exploring the first in chapter 2, I shall focus on the way in which novels embody and generate—to Mr. Gradgrind's chagrin—the activity that he calls "fancy," that ability to imagine nonexistent possibilities, to see one thing as another and one thing in another, to endow a perceived form with a complex life. In chapter 3, I shall focus on the emotions and the various reasons why they have been thought to be a threat to rationality. I shall argue that none of these reasons suffices to dismiss emotions from public reasoning, and that, properly limited and filtered, they provide an irreplaceable kind of guidance for this reasoning. The stance of the literary reader, furthermore, provides us with a powerful filtering device for public emotions. Finally, in chapter 4, I shall turn to the relationship between the literary imagination and public impartiality, especially in the law. Interpreting Walt Whitman's suggestion that the literary artist is "the equalizer of his age and land," I shall suggest a deep connection between "fancy" and democratic equality.

This project raises many questions, some of which I will have to address in context. But I can anticipate at least two of them at this point: the question, Why novels?—and equally important, Which novels?

The "why" question may arise from several different directions. The question, Why novels and not treatises (especially economic treatises) is the central theme of chapter 2. But the reader may also want to know, Why novels and not other forms of narrative, such as histories and biographies? Why novels and not symphonies or films? Finally, even if we are to give pride of place to fictional literary works of some sort, Why novels and not tragedies, or comedies, or lyric poems?[3] It is a little difficult to talk about the "why" before talking about the "what"—before, that is, saying more about the contribution I see the literary works as making. But a few general points will begin to orient the discussion.

Why novels and not histories or biographies? My central subject is the ability to imagine what it is like to live the life of another person who might, given changes in circumstance, be oneself or one of one's loved ones. So my answer to the history question comes straight out of Aristotle. Literary art, he said, is "more philosophical" than history, because history simply shows us "what happened," whereas works of literary art show us "things such as might happen" in a human life.[4] In other words, history simply records what in fact occurred, whether or not it represents a general possibility for human lives. Literature focuses on the possible, inviting its readers to wonder about themselves. Aristotle is correct. Unlike most historical works, literary works typically invite their readers to put themselves in the place of people of many different kinds and to take on their experiences. In their very mode of address to their imagined reader, they convey the sense that there are links of possibility, at least on a very general level, between the characters and the reader. The reader's emotions and imagination are highly active as a result, and it is the nature of this activity, and its relevance for public thinking, that interests me. Historical and biographical works do provide us with empirical information that is essential to good choice. They may in fact also arouse the relevant forms of imaginative activity, if they are written in an inviting narrative style. But to the extent that they promote identification and sympathy in the reader, they resemble literary works. This is especially so if they show the effect of circumstances on the emotions and the inner world—a salient part of the contribution of the literary, as I shall argue.

Another way of putting this point is that good literature is disturbing in a way that history and social science writing frequently are not. Because it summons powerful emotions, it disconcerts and puzzles. It inspires distrust of conventional pieties and exacts a frequently painful confrontation with one's own thoughts and intentions. One may be told many things about people in one's own society and yet keep that knowledge at a distance. Literary works that promote identification and emotional reaction cut through those self-protective stratagems, requiring us to see and to respond to many things that may be difficult to confront—and they make this process palatable by giving us pleasure in the very act of confrontation.[5]

The question, Why literary works and not works in other media—music, say, or dance, or film?—is a deep and fascinating one. Indeed, works in other media frequently have narrative properties and forms of emotional expressiveness that bring them close to the properties of the literary that I shall discuss. Most serious musical works have an expressive emotional content; in some cases (for example, the symphonies of Mahler), it is natural to think of that content as unfolding in narrative form, even if one also knows that any verbal representation of that narrative is at best a halting translation.[6] There are similar analyses to be given in jazz. (All this is relevant to Dickens, since music is, in *Hard Times,* a primary source of the images of sensuousness and play that map the world of the circus.) On the other hand, music's contribution is in its very nature dreamlike and indeterminate in a way that limits its role in public deliberation. Turning to film, recent criticism has shown convincingly that some films have the potential to make contributions similar to those I imagine novels making.[7] And one might plausibly argue that film in our culture has to some extent supplanted the novel as the central morally serious yet popularly engaging narrative medium. I think that this sells short the continuing power of the novel, and I am going to continue in an unapologetic way to discuss the novel as a living form. But I am not reluctant to admit that films may also make contributions to public life in related ways.

Here we have the core of my answer to the question, Why novels and not other literary genres? The novel is a living form and in fact still the central morally serious yet popularly engaging fictional form of our culture. There is much to be said about both classical and Elizabethan tragedy that is closely related to what I shall say here about the novel. (A work such as Sophocles' *Philoctetes* affords essential insights into misfortune and the social benefits of compassion.) But if we are going to speak about contemporary public life, and the ways in which concrete circumstances shape human emotions and aspirations, it seems wise to focus on a genre that is still productive, and in which concrete circumstances that are relevant to our deliberations may be depicted.[8] This will not prevent me from speaking, later on, about lyric poetry as well. But in turning to Walt Whitman, I shall be turning to a poet whose commitment both to narrative and to the concrete depiction of different ways of life brings him into close contact with the novel.

This suggests a more general point about the genre: the novel is concrete to an extent generally unparalleled in other narrative genres. It takes as its theme, we might say, the interaction between general human aspirations and particular forms of social life that either enable or impede those aspirations, shaping them powerfully in the process. Novels (at least realist novels of the sort I shall consider) present persistent forms of human need and desire realized in specific social situations. These situations frequently, indeed usually, differ a good deal from the reader's own. Novels, recognizing this, in general construct and speak to an implicit reader who shares with the characters certain hopes, fears, and general human concerns, and who for that reason is able to form bonds of identification and sympathy with them, but who is also situated elsewhere and needs to be informed about the concrete situation of the characters. In this way, the very structure of the interaction between the text and its imagined reader invites the reader to see how the mutable features of society and circumstance bear on the realization of shared hopes and desires—and also, in fact, on their very structure.

This is beautifully brought out, for example, by the ending of Dickens's *Hard Times*. The narrating voice addresses the reader, saying, "Dear reader! it rests with you and me whether, in our two fields of action, similar things shall be or not." So we have at least three social worlds in play: that of the action of the novel, that of the authorial voice, and that of the reader (itself, in turn, a multiplicity, since the novel does not restrict its address to readers of a single place and time). As a reader (only one among many, and concretely situated in my own sphere), I notice that the lives of factory workers in my own society differ in some ways from the lives of the workers of Coketown; in other ways, however, they do not differ as much as I might wish. I assess these conditions with reference to certain very general norms of human flourishing that are built into my compassionate response, into its judgment of what is serious damage to a life and what is not. I notice that access to divorce in my own society is easier and less class-divided than it was in the time of Stephen Blackpool, but that in other respects gender relations and problems connected with marriage and the family have not changed, or have perhaps in some respects grown more difficult. I notice, too, that there are still some couples in my society who cannot marry at all when they would like to avail themselves of the benefits of marriage. Again, I assess all this with reference to certain views about human freedom and human functioning that I take to have universal significance, at least at a high level of generality. I cannot read as an immersed participant without bringing some such views to bear; they are implicit in the very emotions with which I respond.

As I read, I notice that Gradgrind economics has an even greater hold over the political and intellectual life of my society than it did over the society known to Dickens's characters, or to the narrating voice in his novel. I notice that the type of cost-benefit analysis favored by economics has become so familiar in public policy that it is taken for granted; at the same time, public servants are less and less likely to be readers of literature, where they would discover a more complex vision of human life. And I wonder about these changes, and how they bear on what I, as a concerned citizen, should be doing with my time. In all these ways and many others, I am invited to think about human flourishing and to see how "men and women more or less like" myself (Dickens's way of describing the people his characters encounter when *they* read novels) have lived differently from the way I now live, on account of things that might be otherwise.

This play back and forth between the general and the concrete is, I claim, built into the very structure of the genre, in its mode of address to its readers. In this way, the novel constructs a paradigm of a style of ethical reasoning that is context-specific without being relativistic, in which we get potentially universalizable concrete prescriptions by bringing a general idea of human flourishing to bear on a concrete situation, which we are invited to enter through the imagination. This is a valuable form of public reasoning, both within a single culture and across cultures. For the most part, the genre fosters it to a greater degree than classical tragic dramas, short stories, or lyric poems.

I have imagined the reader as concretely situated, but different readers, of course, have different concrete situations. Different readers will legitimately notice different things about a novel, both interpreting and also assessing it in varied ways. This naturally suggests a further development of the idea of public reasoning as novel-reading: that the reasoning involved is not only context-specific but also, when well done, comparative, evolving in conversation with other readers whose perceptions challenge or supplement one's own. This is the idea of "co-duction," elaborated by Wayne Booth in his excellent book *The Company We Keep: An Ethics of Fiction*.[9] Booth argues that the act of reading and assessing what one has read is ethically valuable precisely because it is constructed in a manner that demands both immersion and critical conversation, comparison of what one has read both with one's own unfolding experience and with the responses and arguments of other readers. If we think of reading in this way, as combining one's own absorbed imagining with periods of more detached (and interactive) critical scrutiny, we can already begin to see why we might find in it an activity well suited to public reasoning in a democratic society.

There is one more feature of novel-reading that needs recognition at the outset: the novel's interest in the ordinary. As readers of *Hard Times*, we visit a schoolroom, a middle-class home, a circus, a working-class home, the office of a manager, the factory in which working people toil, an abandoned mineshaft in which many working people have met their death. Not one of these places would have been judged fit for inclusion in the tragedies of Aeschylus and Sophocles or of Corneille and Racine.[10] Even in political history and biography, the lives of the insignificant many appear, on the whole, only as classes or statistics, not too differently from the way they figure in the books Mr. Gradgrind recommends. But in reading Dickens's story, we embrace the ordinary. It is made an object of our keenest interest and sympathy. We visit these places as involved friends, concerned about what is happening in them. This was a distinctive mark of the genre from its inception, in England above all, and a great part of its connection to the rise of democracy.[11] At each stage in the development of the genre, we find self-referential moments that signal this feature to the reader. When Louisa goes to visit Stephen Blackpool halfway through *Hard Times*, Dickens emphasizes the fact that she had never before known anything concrete about the lives of factory workers, having learned of their existence only as abstract statistics. Readers are invited to notice that their own experience as novel-readers has been very different from hers. Similarly, when Richard Wright's well-meaning liberal, Mary Dalton, exclaims that she knows nothing of the lives of people ten blocks from her house, Wright's readers are invited to recall that their own experience began in Bigger Thomas's tenement, as witnesses to Bigger's assault on a foot-long rat. In Forster's *Maurice*, characters repeatedly portray the homosexual as a deviant profligate being, in all respects unlike themselves. Forster's reader has come to know that Maurice is in most respects a boringly ordinary middle-class stockbroker, whose sexual fantasies focus on the image of a loving friend. The novel determinedly introduces its reader to that which is in a way common and close at hand—but which is often, in its significant strangeness, the object of profound ignorance and emotional refusal.

This brings us to the question, Which novels? I shall argue that the genre itself, on account of some general features of its structure, generally constructs empathy and compassion in ways highly relevant to citizenship. Adam Smith was correct when he found in the experience of readership a model of the attitudes and emotions of the judicious spectator. But of course there is no "genre itself"; there are only novels, works that share no single core of features over the centuries, though they are connected by a network of overlapping resemblances. It does seem to me significant that one needs to subvert central properties of the tradition (removing invitations to investigate the psychology and history of the characters that are as "essential" as any elements in the genre) in order to do away with qualitative distinctions and individuality, with compassion, even with mercy. In chapter 4, discussing Richard Wright's *Native Son*, I shall return to this point. But clearly, too, not every work that has many common features of the genre will prove equally valuable for citizenship. Wayne Booth's analysis shows graphically what we all know: that many popular works entice the reader through crude sentiments and the evocation of fantasies that may involve the dehumanization of others.[12] Ethical assessment of the novels themselves, in conversation both with other readers and with the arguments of moral and political theory, is therefore necessary if the contribution of novels is to be politically fruitful. We are seeking, overall, the best fit between our considered moral and political judgments and the insights offered by our reading. Reading can lead us to alter some of our standing judgments, but it is also the case that these judgments can cause us to reject some experiences of reading as deforming or pernicious.[13]

I have chosen to focus on the realist Anglo-American novel, and in particular on a group of novels with social and political themes. The second chapter will focus on *Hard Times*, which I have chosen for its attention to the relationship between the literary imagination and its economic adversaries, and for its investigation of the role of "fancy." Although there are good reasons to criticize some aspects of Dickens's portrayal of society, I believe that his novel contains (in its form, as well as in the statements made within it) valuable insights into the power of the imagination in politics, insights not unconnected with the novel's metaphorical and linguistic richness.

But people cannot learn everything they need to learn as citizens simply by reading works set in a distant place and time, no matter how universally applicable many of those works' insights may be. Reading Dickens shows us many things about compassion; it does not show us the very particular ways in which our society inhibits our compassion for people of different race, gender, or sexuality. Nor does it show the ways in which social inequality and hatred form and deform the emotional lives of the hated. Therefore, in chapter 4, speaking about social equality, I shall turn to Wright and to E. M. Forster to investigate these questions.

Two points should now be emphasized. First, although I shall emphasize *Hard Times*'s critique of economics, I do not regard my own literary investigation as antiscientific or as involving a call for the dismissal of economic science. That would be a ludicrous proposal. It was not even proposed by Dickens, who said that we should come upon "Reason" (by which he meant formal scientific reasoning) "through the tender light of Fancy," not that we should confine ourselves to "Fancy" and live in the circus all our lives. Moreover, Dickens was more globally skeptical of economics than he should have been. His hostility to formal mathematical modeling prevented him from seeing that problems for which he sought a solution in private charity might in fact be susceptible of a public institutional solution.

My proposal is a more modest one, that economic science should be built on human data of the sort novels such as Dickens's reveal to the imagination, that economic science should seek a more complicated and philosophically adequate set of foundations. As will be seen in my discussion of recent economic-philosophical work on the quality of life in chapter 2, there is every reason to think that an approach that includes the sort of insight I claim to find in literature permits a kind of modeling and measurement more predictively fruitful, and more capable of giving good guidance to policy, than the types otherwise available in economic science. But of course such insights should not displace the workings of economic science, which can do many things that the imaginations of individuals, without such formal models, cannot do, giving us, among other things, a practical sense of how certain goals that the imagination may present to us—less unemployment, lower prices, in general a better quality of life—might be accomplished.

Second, an emphasis on the literary imagination is not meant to displace moral and political theory or to substitute emotions for principled arguments. Any such interpretation of my proposal would be profoundly contrary to its intention and spirit. Indeed, as will be seen in chapter 3, the reader's emotions are implicitly evaluative and rest, therefore, on a theory of the good. As I have already suggested, discussing Booth, this theory ought to be tested against the moral and political theories philosophy has proposed, both within each reader's internal reflection and in conversation with other readers. By itself it is not complete and might even prove misleading. In themselves, the reader's responses already point in the direction of some political theories rather than others: they prove difficult to square with utilitarianism and are far more at home with aspects of Kantian and Aristotelian views of the human being. But the subtle differences between those theories need to be thrashed out by philosophical arguments. Novel-reading all by itself will not supply those arguments, which might at some points lead us to reject the insights of our reading itself.

I make two claims, then, for the reader's experience: first, that it provides insights that should play a role (though not as uncriticized foundations) in the construction of an adequate moral and political theory; second, that it develops moral capacities without which citizens will not succeed in making reality out of the normative conclusions of any moral or political theory, however excellent. As I said in the preface, novel-reading will not give us the whole story about social justice, but it can be a bridge both to a vision of justice and to the social enactment of that vision.

2

Fancy

"Bitzer," said Thomas Gradgrind. *"Your definition of a horse."*

"Quadruped. Graminivorous. Forty teeth, namely twenty-four grinders, four eye-teeth, and twelve incisive. Sheds coat in the spring; in marshy countries, sheds hoofs, too. Hoofs hard, but requiring to be shod with iron. Age known by marks in mouth." Thus (and much more) Bitzer.

"Now girl number twenty," said Mr Gradgrind. *"You know what a horse is."*

All the fathers could dance upon rolling casks, stand upon bottles, catch knives and balls, twirl hand-basins, ride upon anything, jump over everything, and stick at nothing. All the mothers could (and did) dance, upon the slack wire and the tight-rope, and perform rapid acts on barebacked steeds; none of them were at all particular in respect of showing their legs; and one of them, alone in a Greek chariot, drove six in hand into every town they came to.

Charles Dickens, *Hard Times*

Nothing but Facts

Dickens's *Hard Times* contains a normative vision of a scientific political economics and of the scientific political imagination. It presents this norm, to be sure, as a target of withering satirical attack. But since the attack is a deep attack, the novel both describes the satirical target with insight and shows the deeper significance of what is still today very often taught as normative in public policy-making, in sociology and political science, in welfare and development economics—and recently, even in the law, where the law-and-economics movement exercises an increasing hold over the education of future lawyers and judges.

The utilitarian rational-choice models that are in use today derive, ultimately, from the utilitarianism known to Mr. Gradgrind, though with some important differences that I shall shortly describe. The most common models involve four elements: commensurability, aggregation, maximizing, and exogenous preferences.

By *commensurability*, I mean that rational choice, in these models, involves regarding all the valuable things under consideration as measurable on a single scale that itself exhibits differences only of quantity, not quality. This may be because, as in nineteenth-century classical utilitarianism, there is an explicit commitment to a monistic theory of value (all the valuable things are valuable because they contain some one thing that itself varies only in quantity), or because, despite the plurality of values, there is an argument that shows that a single metric adequately captures what is valuable in them all.[1] (It may also be because, although the theorist does not believe that the single metric captures what is really valuable, it seems a sufficient basis for modeling choice for predictive purposes. That role for commensurability escapes some of the criticisms I shall make, and I shall return to it at the end.)

By *aggregation*, I mean that a social result is obtained by pooling the data about and from individual lives, without regarding the boundaries between lives as especially salient for the purposes of choice.[2]

By the commitment to *maximizing*, I mean the commitment to see both individual and social rationality as aimed at getting as large an amount of something as possible, whether that something be wealth, or the satisfaction of preferences and desires, or pleasure, or that elusive item, utility.

Finally, the theory assumes that people's preferences are *exogenous*—in other words, that for economic purposes they can be taken as given. Frequently, though not always, this is associated with the view that preferences are simply a raw material for personal or social choice and are not themselves the product of social choices.[3]

These assumptions give utilitarianism its characteristic view of persons. As Amartya Sen and Bernard Williams vividly express the point: "Essentially, utilitarianism sees persons as locations of their respective utilities—as the sites at which such activities as desiring and having pleasure and pain take place. Once note has been taken of the person's utility, utilitarianism has no further direct interest in any information about him. . . . Persons do not count as individuals in this any more than individual petrol tanks do in the analysis of the national consumption of petroleum."[4] In other words, neither the qualitative distinctions between persons (beyond the sheer quantity of utility they generate) nor, ultimately, the boundaries between them (they are all just containers of utility or sites at which utility is realized), nor their freedom of choice (for utility is usually defined in a way that makes no essential reference to agency) will be salient from the point of view of the utilitarian account.

Utilitarian rational-choice models are used for various purposes. Some of these purposes are *explanatory/predictive:* the economist claims, using the model, that if certain actions are chosen, certain results will follow. Other uses are *normative:* conduct that does not conform to the model is criticized as irrational or substandard for that reason, and the model is used to guide the selection of public policies. Cutting across this distinction is another one, to which I shall later return, between theorists who give some substantive account of the item, for example, utility, that is to be maximized and therefore make claims that are specific and testable, and others who simply assume that actual behavior reveals preferences and who therefore make claims about the role of behavior in maximizing preference-satisfaction that are extremely difficult to test.

Classical utilitarianism and contemporary rational-choice models appear to diverge sharply. From this common basis, the classical theories of Bentham and Sidgwick focus on normative rather than explanatory uses of utility and, within the normative project, on a radical idea, according to which the proper aim of both personal and social choice is the maximization of the sum total of (or, in some versions, the average of) human happiness, usually understood as pleasure or satisfaction. This, it will easily be seen, is an extremely exigent and revisionary moral theory. It holds that in every one of my choices I should prefer the option that is best for human life as a whole. If I am a comfortable middle-class person, this theory is likely to make greater demands on me for altruism and self-sacrifice than most other familiar moral theories. It requires me to count myself as just one among the human beings in the world, and not to give preference to my own friends and family, my own goals and projects. Classical utilitarians do not suggest that most people currently behave this way; they are aware that they do not. I believe the emphasis on the equal worth of persons is an extremely valuable aspect of the classical utilitarian ideal; as we shall see, it is one that Dickens's novel to a great extent endorses.

By contrast, contemporary rational-choice theorists usually focus on explanatory/predictive rather than normative claims; they claim to provide models that enable us to predict behavior, not to give directions for change in behavior. And their descriptive theory, far from focusing on altruism, holds that the end of individual rational choice is always the maximization of the satisfaction of individual self-interest. Altruism can be accommodated in these behavioral assumptions only if it is understood instrumentally— doing a good turn for someone else in some way helps me to maximize my utility or my preference-satisfaction.[5] One might then suppose that the contemporary theory is ruling irrational the very sort of altruistic choice that the classical theory holds up as paradigmatic of the (normatively) rational.

There is much truth in this; and to that extent *Hard Times* will appear to the modern reader to have a divided target, since it directs its energies against the shared assumptions of the two theories, sometimes focusing on the normative social goals of the classical theory and sometimes on the behavioral assumptions of something like the contemporary theory. But the two theories are in fact closer than this account has indicated, for the classical theory, in addition to its normative account of choice, needs a descriptive account of the ways in which people really do choose most of the time. The theory neither expects nor even desires that most people should think like normative utilitarians in all of their choices; well-known difficulties flow from the hypothesis that they might.[6] So the theory needs, in addition to its exigent norm, an account of how most people choose in daily life; and Dickens is not implausible in suggesting that the model of maximizing the satisfaction of personal interests and preferences is one that a Gradgrind economist might consistently develop. In fact, this is pretty much what Jeremy Bentham, founder of the classical theory, assumed to be true of people. On the other side, contemporary rational-choice theory has its own normative dimension. Some writers in the law-and-economics movement, for example, hold that the aim of rational social choice is the maximization of society's wealth—a goal that is understood to be promoted, on the whole, by the self-interested choices of descriptively rational agents. The goal of wealth-maximization is a normative goal, though this is not always made clear: thus, choices can be and are criticized as ill done when they do not promote that goal.[7] While not precisely the same as the goal of classical utilitarians such as Bentham and Sidgwick (for even a utilitarian will admit that wealth is not equivalent to happiness), it is a goal that has a close relation to theirs and makes (or so it would seem) similar demands on the individual. In many other ways, contemporary models propose norms for social choice and the direction of public policy.

The utilitarian picture of human beings and of rationality is familiar enough in theory. What makes the utilitarian norm appear so odd to the reader of Dickens's novel is that it is taken seriously all the way down, so to speak: understood not just as a way of writing up reports, but as a way of dealing with people in daily encounters; not just as a way of doing economics, but as a way of defining a horse or talking to a child; not just as a way of appearing professionally respectable, but as a commitment that determines the whole content of one's personal and social life. But since this norm does in fact claim to be a standard of rationality, and not just a handy professional tool, and since, if it is really a norm, it also seems fair to ask people to abide by it consistently, it also seems perfectly fair to ask what people who really and thoroughly saw the world in the way this norm recommends would be like, and whether such a vision is a complete one. And it seems reasonable, too, to suppose that the personal vision and conduct of committed social scientists is actually influenced at least to some extent by the content of the norm their science upholds, by the habits of perception and recognition it encourages. So in examining utilitarianism, we want to learn something about what we do to people by holding it up as a norm and what we can expect from people so treated.[8]

Moreover, especially in the burgeoning literature on the economics of nonmarket behavior, we increasingly find analyses that seem to the noneconomic reader just as peculiar as the teachings of the Gradgrind school. Consider, for example, a recent entirely serious article entitled "The Deadweight Loss of Christmas," arguing that noncash gifts are less efficient than cash gifts and that the practice of present-giving generates four billion dollars in annual "deadweight losses."[9] Consider, too, the following Gradgrindian account of sexual choices from Richard Posner's much-discussed *Sex and Reason:*

The different *types* of cost that sex involves, and the major factors that bear
on these costs, have now to be considered. One is the cost of search. It is
zero for masturbation, considered as a solitary activity, which is why it is
the cheapest of sexual practices. (The qualification is important: "mutual
masturbation," heterosexual or homosexual, is a form of nonvaginal intercourse, and its search costs are positive.) . . . Men will incur considerable
search costs for a call girl—and even higher ones, of course, for a mistress or
a wife—but few or none for the lowest quality of sexual services, which therefore are provided by streetwalkers, the zero-search-cost prostitutes. Analo-
gously, the lowest-quality goods are consumed at home, not shipped at all.[10]

These peculiar ways of talking can be seriously defended. I shall later
consider the plausible objection that the rational-choice approach is not intended to model the way people really do think and act, but only to provide
an "as if" model for predicting choice. But I shall argue that this objection,
while partly successful, not only does not detract from, but actually en-
hances, the critical contribution of a novel such as *Hard Times*. Let us, however, first explore, with the novel, the strangeness of these ways of talking
about human beings and ask why they are so strange.

What I am about to say here may seem in some respects obvious, for it is
part of the novel's design that the economist's way of thinking, seen in the
full context of daily life, should look extremely strange, and the opposing
way natural. But Dickens's economic opponent is not a straw man: it is a
conception that even now dominates much of our public life, in a form not
very different from the form presented in this novel. If one looks to the complicated modifications of utilitarianism available in moral philosophy, the
satire of *Hard Times* can appear insufficiently subtle.[11] But the economic version of utilitarian rational-choice theory usually contains few of these philosophical subtleties, and it has far more influence than do the philosophical
versions. It dominates not only economic thought and practice, but also—
given the prestige of economics within the social sciences—a great deal of
writing in other social sciences as well, where "rational-choice theory" is
taken to be equivalent to utilitarian rational-choice theory as practiced in
neoclassical economics. Public policy-makers turn to these norms to find a
principled, orderly way of making decisions. Economic approaches have
been widely influential even in areas that might initially seem most uneco-
nomic, such as the analysis of the family and of sexuality.[12] And the allure

of the theory's elegant simplicity is so great that it is having an increasing influence even in the law, although much of the legal tradition has endorsed a more complicated picture of practical reasoning, closely related to the one that this chapter will defend. Recently the theory has even made its way into literary studies, where the prestige of neoclassical economics, Chicago style, is invoked in defense of a broad application of its behavioral theory to all areas of human life.[13] The reader who has no familiarity with the opposing position may turn to Gary Becker's writing on the family, or Richard Posner's on a variety of topics, in order to get a fuller sense of its ways of speaking about persons. Posner's and Becker's views are extreme, but only in the sense that, like this novel, they apply across the board a theory that economics treats as applicable to rational choice in general. If that theory is indeed an adequate account of rationality, they are right to do so, and we are justified in examining their works as tests of the theory's vision.[14] Proponents of such economic approaches have made very large claims on their behalf: that "economics is applied rationality," even that "all of man's deliberative, forward-looking behavior follows the principles of economics."[15] Those claims should be carefully scrutinized. In order to begin this scrutiny, let us now turn to Mr. Gradgrind, who—unlike most of his cousins on the contemporary scene—at least ends by expressing remorse, revealing in the process a certain human complexity.

The reader should be aware from the beginning that my criticism (like the novel's) is directed toward a particular conception of economic science, not toward the idea of economic science itself, and certainly not toward the idea that abstract theories of a scientific sort can be crucial to the good conduct of public life. The criticism is allied, as will become plain, to an alternative conception of economic science and economic rationality that is itself thoroughly scientific, that claims in fact to be more scientific in the sense of being more true and more precise, and that is allied to philosophical theorizing in much the way that economic utilitarianism is allied to philosophical utilitarian theories—although its favored philosophers are Kant, Rawls, Mill, Smith, Dewey, and Aristotle rather than Bentham and Sidgwick.

"In this life, we want nothing but Facts, sir; nothing but Facts." This famous demand, announced in the Gradgrind schoolroom in the opening chapter of the novel (a chapter entitled "The One Thing Needful"), states the essence of the Gradgrind philosophy. And the novel shortly characterizes it further, speaking for Mr. Gradgrind in the hard, blunt confrontational sentences that seem well suited to express the quality of his mind:

> Thomas Gradgrind, sir. A man of realities. A man of fact and calculations. A man who proceeds upon the principle that two and two are four, and nothing over, and who is not to be talked into allowing for anything over. Thomas Gradgrind, sir—peremptorily Thomas—Thomas Gradgrind. With a rule and a pair of scales, and the multiplication table always in his pocket, sir, ready to weigh and measure any parcel of human nature, and tell you exactly what it comes to. It is a mere question of figures, a case of simple arithmetic.

Gradgrind's economics claims to be a science, to offer facts in place of idle fancy, objectivity in place of mere subjective impressions, the precision of mathematical calculation instead of the intractable elusiveness of qualitative distinctions. "The reason is (as you know)," he remarks to his friend Bounderby, "the only faculty to which education should be addressed." Gradgrind economics claims proudly to approach the world with reason rather than sentiment, and with the detached theoretical and calculative power of the mathematical intellect, rather than any more qualitative type of reasoned deliberation. Gradgrind intellect sees the heterogeneous furniture of the world, human beings included, as so many surfaces or "parcels" to be weighed and measured.

In this brief description we see four aspects of the economic-utilitarian mind, neatly encapsulated.[16] First, it reduces qualitative differences to quantitative differences. Instead of Louisa, Tom, Stephen, Rachael, in all of their qualitative diversity, their historical particularity, we have simply so-and-so-many quantifiable "parcels of human nature." This effacement of qualitative difference is accomplished, we see, by a process of abstraction from all in people that is not easily funneled into mathematical formulae; so this mind, in order to measure what it measures, attends only to an abstract and highly general version of the human being, rather than to the diverse concreteness with which the novel confronts us from the start—Sissy Jupe's dark shining eyes and Bitzer's cold little pale eyes, the bald head of teacher M'Choakumchild shining "like the crust of a plum pie," the dark hair of pupil Sissy, who "received a deeper and more lustrous colour from the sun when it shone upon her."[17] We see this abstracting mathematical mind at work in the Gradgrind school's treatment of its students, called by number ("Girl number twenty") rather than by name, and seen as an "inclined plane of little vessels then and there arranged in order, ready to have imperial gallons of facts poured into them until they were full to the brim."[18] We see it at work in the treatment of the workers of Coketown as so-and-so-many "hands and stomachs," as "teeming myriads" whose destinies can be reckoned on a slate, their qualitative differences as irrelevant as those of "ants and beetles" "passing to and from their nests."

Second, the Gradgrind mind, bent on calculation, is determined to aggregate the data gained about and from individual lives, arriving at a picture of total or average utility that effaces personal separateness as well as qualitative difference. The individual is not even as distinct as a distinct countable insect, for in Mr. Gradgrind's calculation, the person becomes simply an input into a complex mathematical operation that treats the social unit as a single large system in which the preferences and satisfactions of all are combined and melded. Thus, in Louisa's education, the working classes become

> Something to be worked so much and paid so much, and there ended; something to be infallibly settled by laws of supply and demand; something that blundered against those laws, and floundered into difficulty; something that was a little pinched when wheat was dear, and overate itself when wheat was cheap; something that increased at such a rate of percentage, and yielded such another percentage of crime, and such another percentage of pauperism; something wholesale, of which vast fortunes were made; something that occasionally rose like the sea, and did some harm and waste (chiefly to itself), and fell again; this she knew the Coketown hands to be. But, she had scarcely thought more of separating them into units, than of separating the sea itself into its component drops.

Lives are drops in an undemarcated ocean, and the question of how the group is doing is a question whose economic resolution requires effacing the unbridgeable separateness between one person's misery and another's satisfaction.[19] For related reasons, the question requires treating agency and freedom as peripheral, for the individual is seen as a container of satisfactions, whose own active choice is irrelevant to the theory, except insofar as choice is itself a source of satisfaction.[20]

Mr. Gradgrind does not perfectly efface separateness and agency in his school, where students retain their individual levels of performance, their abilities to think and speak as separate centers of choice, and even some measure of qualitative distinctness. He does not achieve this goal perfectly, we are bound to observe, in his relation to himself, for his internal rhetoric, in the passage cited above, insists on the separateness and the qualitative difference of his own mind from those of others: "You might hope to get some other nonsensical belief into the head of George Gradgrind, or Augustus Gradgrind, or John Gradgrind, or Joseph Gradgrind (all supposititious, nonexistent persons), but into the head of Thomas Gradgrind—no sir!" It is a subtle point in the novel that the measure of personal autonomy and self-respect that Mr. Gradgrind wishes to claim for himself requires him to view himself with a distinctness denied in his calculations—and even to indulge in a rare bit of (however crude) fiction-making.

But within his immediate family, he fares better, for he does manage, most of the time, to perceive his own children in more or less the way that his theory recommends.[21] When Louisa, in inner agony about her impending marriage to Bounderby, bursts out: "'Father, I have often thought that life is very short,'" her baffled father replies:

> "It is short, no doubt, my dear. Still, the average duration of human life is proved to have increased of late years. The calculations of various life assurance and annuity offices, among other figures which cannot go wrong, have established the fact."
>
> "I speak of my own life, father."
>
> "O indeed? Still," said Mr. Gradgrind, "I need not point out to you, Louisa, that it is governed by the laws which govern lives in the aggregate."[22]

And in one of the novel's most chilling and brilliant moments, we see what it can be like to see oneself through the eyes of the Gradgrind theory. Mrs. Gradgrind, subservient and with an always fragile sense both of her own qualitative distinctness and of her separate boundaries, her separate agency, lies on what will soon be her deathbed. "'Are you in pain, dear mother?'" asks Louisa. The answer comes back. "'I think there's a pain somewhere in the room,' said Mrs. Gradgrind, 'but I couldn't positively say that I have got it.'" Political economy sees only pains and satisfactions and their general location:

it does not see persons as bounded centers of satisfaction, far less as agents whose active planning is essential to the humanness of whatever satisfaction they will achieve. Mrs. Gradgrind has learned her lesson well.

If we return now to the initial description of Mr. Gradgrind, we see in it a third feature of the Gradgrind-economical mind: its determination to find, by some sort of "sum-ranking" or maximizing procedure, a clear and precise solution for any human problem.[23] Mr. Gradgrind, we recall, is prepared "to weigh and measure any parcel of human nature, and tell you exactly what it comes to." And his study, later on, is described as a "charmed apartment" in which "the most complicated social questions were cast up, got into exact totals, and finally settled." Because it has from the start cast the human data into "tabular form," the economic mind finds it easy to view the lives of human beings as a problem in (relatively elementary) mathematics that has a definite solution—ignoring the mystery and complexity within each life, in its puzzlement and pain about its choices, in its tangled loves, in its attempt to grapple with the mysterious and awful fact of its own mortality.[24] The cheerful fact-calculating mind plays round the surfaces of these lives, as if it had no need to look within, as if, indeed, it "could settle all their destinies on a slate."

The idea that "simple arithmetic" can solve any human problem has a pervasive influence in the Gradgrind education. Gradgrind children are taught from an early age to approach the world of nature without any sense of mystery or awe. Thus the "good student" Bitzer's definition of a horse, which gives a remarkably flat and abstract description of the surface features of that animal, refusing to imagine either its own complex form of life or its significance in the lives of humans who love and care for horses. So, too, with human lives. Mr. Gradgrind does not even understand the significance of his own child's outburst, when she speaks obscurely of a fire that bursts forth at night and wonders about the shortness of her life. How much less, then, does he feel a sense of wonder before the distant human beings who work in the factories of Coketown. In one of the most striking incursions of a first-person voice into this novel, Dickens describes, and criticizes, this habit of mind:

> So many hundred Hands in this Mill; so many hundred horse Steam Power.
> It is known, to the force of a single pound weight, what the engine will do;
> but, not all the calculators of the National Debt can tell me the capacity

for good or evil, for love or hatred, for patriotism or discontent, for the decomposition of virtue into vice, or the reverse, at any single moment in the soul of one of these its quiet servants, with the composed faces and the regulated actions. There is no mystery in it; there is an unfathomable mystery in the meanest of them, for ever. Supposing we were to reserve our arithmetic for material objects, and to govern these awful unknown quantities by other means!

If economic policy-making does not acknowledge the complexities of the inner moral life of each human being, its strivings and perplexities, its complicated emotions, its efforts at understanding and its terror, if it does not distinguish in its descriptions between a human life and a machine, then we should regard with suspicion its claim to govern a nation of human beings; and we should ask ourselves whether, having seen us as little different from inanimate objects, it might not be capable of treating us with a certain obtuseness.

This brings us directly to the fourth characteristic of economic rationality with which the novel acquaints us. Seeing human beings as counters in a mathematical game, and refusing to see their mysterious inner world, the Gradgrind philosophy is able to adopt a theory of human motivation that is elegant and simple, well suited for the game of calculation, but whose relation to the more complicated laws that govern the inner world of a human being should be viewed with skepticism. In accordance with Gradgrind's view of himself as a down-to-earth, realistic man, a man of cold, hard fact rather than airy fancy, the theory has an air of hard-nosed realism about it, suggesting the unmasking of pleasant but empty fictions. Human beings, this unsentimental view teaches, are all motivated by self-interest in all of their actions.[25] The all-too-perfect Gradgrind pupil Bitzer, at the novel's end, reveals the principle on which he was raised. As the chastened Mr. Gradgrind attempts to appeal to his gratitude and love, Bitzer cuts in:

> "I beg your pardon for interrupting you, sir," returned Bitzer; "but I am sure you know that the whole social system is a question of self-interest. What you must always appeal to, is a person's self-interest. It's your only hold. We are so constituted. I was brought up in that catechism when I was very young, sir, as you are aware."

Bitzer refuses to acknowledge even those residual motivations of love and altruism that now deeply grip the heart of Mr. Gradgrind himself. Self-interest is the philosophy on which he was raised. And this philosophy leads to odd and implausible interpretations of the world.

Earlier in the novel, when Sissy Jupe's father, an aging circus clown, has left her, and her own first inclination is to impute to him altruistic motives, projects for her good, the industrialist Bounderby will have none of it. She had better know, he says, the hard bad facts of her situation: she has been abandoned; her father has simply pleased himself and run off. The novel pointedly leaves this particular case unresolved. We know that Jupe is depressed because of his failure to make the audience laugh, and we know that he intensely loves his child; we never do know how these motives interact in determining his choice. For this very reason, Jupe's case points up different behavioral assumptions in its interpreters, different ways of construing the world. The novel as a whole convinces the reader (and Mr. Gradgrind) that Gradgrind is wrong to deny the possibility of genuinely altruistic and other-regarding action. But if this other possibility exists, then Bounderby has construed Sissy's situation hastily, and also ungenerously. The suggestion is that the economist's habit of reducing everything to calculation, combined with the need for an extremely simple theory of human action, produces a tendency to see calculation everywhere, rather than commitment and sympathy. "Every inch of the existence of mankind, from birth to death, was to be a bargain across a counter."[26] This tendency leads to crude analysis, and frequently to error. Even when it does not lead to error, it leads to an ungenerous perception of people and events. And, worst of all, taught from an early age, it produces pupils in its own image.

One further aspect of the behavioral theory now needs emphasis. Gradgrind economics, like its contemporary relatives, regards the interests and preferences of individuals as simply given, as inputs into the theory of social choice, rather than as socially mutable features of persons that can themselves be shaped by social arrangements. Thus factory owner Bounderby simply assumes that his workers will want the luxuries that he wants. He can't imagine that they are so deprived of basic freedoms and necessities that "to be fed on turtle soup and venison, with a gold spoon," would not be even a happy fantasy, much less a project. He has no curiosity about the ways in which misery affects aspiration and even impedes the capacity for robust discontent. Thus Bounderby, again, attributes to Sissy's father the selfish disregard of family that has marked his own rise to power, not re-

flecting on the ways in which differences of moral education produce different preferences. Dickens's novel, by contrast, persistently tracks the social
origins, formations, and deformations of desire in a way that strikingly antic-
ipates some of the most interesting recent criticisms of economic rationality.[27] Again, there might in some circumstances be reasons for the economist
to ignore these facts, but one should begin by acknowledging their depth
and prevalence.

In short, the claim of Gradgrind economics to present all and only the
facts of human life needs to be viewed with skepticism, if by "facts" we mean
"truths." And its claim to stand for "reason" must also be viewed with skepticism, if by "reason" we mean a faculty that is self-critical and committed
to truth. For the "facts" of political economy are actually reductive and incomplete perceptions, and its "reason" is a dogmatic operation of intellect
that looks, frequently, both incomplete and unreliable. The fact-finding intellect plays around the surfaces of objects, not even obtaining very adequate
perceptual data—Mr. Gradgrind's study is compared to an astronomical
observatory without windows, where the astronomer arranges the world
"solely by pen, ink, and paper" determined to perceive only those abstract
features of people and situations that can easily be translated into economic
calculations. From its own point of view, the Gradgrind mind has positive
motivations for this way of proceeding—its determination to be realistic
and not sentimental, its determination to be exact, and even its determination not to be biased in favor of what is near at hand. (Thus Mr. Gradgrind
reflects that Louisa "would have been self-willed . . . but for her bringing-
up.") The novel permits us to see these positive goals. Its very sentences
express a commitment to be detached, realistic, and unbiased—in their
blunt, square shape, their syntactical plainness, their hard sound and
rhythm. (We must, however, note that the prose the novel imputes to the
Gradgrind imagination is far more expressive, more succinct, more rhyth-
mical, more pleasing in its odd squareness, than the flat, unexpressive,
jargon-laden prose that is actually used by many economists of the Gradgrind type. Dickens has been able to make Mr. Gradgrind a lively character
in a readable novel only by to this extent changing him.)

But, the novel shows, in its determination to see only what can enter into
utilitarian calculations, the economic mind is blind: blind to the qualitative
richness of the perceptible world; to the separateness of its people, to their

inner depths, their hopes and loves and fears; blind to what it is like to live a human life and to try to endow it with a human meaning. Blind, above all, to the fact that human life is something mysterious and extremely complicated, something that demands to be approached with faculties of mind and resources of language that are suited to the expression of that complexity. In the name of science, the wonder that illuminates and prompts the deepest science has been jettisoned.[28] In the name of taking each person's pain seriously—the noblest motivation in the birth of utilitarianism—we have a view that cannot adequately fathom any person's pain in its social context or see it as the pain of a separate person. If the job of science is to record and grapple with all the relevant facts, the Gradgrind theory is inadequate science, since many of the relevant human facts are simply not noticed.

Mere Fables about Men and Women

Let us now ask how Dickens's novel differs from the utilitarian texts mentioned in it, with their "tabular statements" measuring social welfare. How does it shape its reader's desires and expectations?[29] What aspects of the world does it recognize as salient? What vision of human beings and human life does the reader take on in the act of reading? We must begin with the most obvious facts: not taking for granted the fact that we are reading a work in a different genre, but asking about the features of the genre itself, and how they form the reader's imagination.

First of all, then, we are reading a story. This story puts before us characters—men and women in some ways like ourselves. It represents these characters as very distinct one from another, endowing them with physical and moral attributes that make it possible for us to distinguish every one from every other. We are made to attend to their ways of moving and talking, the shapes of their bodies, the expressions on their faces, the sentiments of their hearts. The inner life of each is displayed as having psychological depth and complexity. We see that as humans they share certain common problems and common hopes—and yet, as well, that each confronts these in his or her own way, in his or her concrete circumstances with the resources of his or her history. Even the utilitarians Bounderby and Gradgrind are completely human figures, for their abstract philosophy emerges from an inner world with which it is not always—as we have begun to see—in harmony. We see the novel's abstract deliberations, then, as issuing in each case from a concrete human life, and as expressing only a part of that life's inner richness. And although we do not always have extended and explicit access to a character's internal world, we are always invited to wonder about it—imagining the motives that drive Bounderby to deny his origins and Mrs. Sparsit to pursue Louisa, imagining later on, with warmer sympathy, the turmoil in the heart of Mr. Gradgrind as he greets the collapse of his system with humble expressions of remorse. We wonder how to interpret their actions, and we wonder with a mixture of sympathy and criticism that is likely to vary to some extent from reader to reader, as attitudes do toward actual people in life. (Thus we can argue about what the correct interpretation of some element of the novel might be, and how justified our sympathies have been, without losing the fundamental concern that draws us together as readers.)

All these things the novel, in its very ways of speaking to its reader, recognizes as salient, as worthy of attention and concern. This we take for granted, since we know what it is to read a novel. But we should not take it for granted. We should be aware at all times how our attention and desire are directed, and how differently from their direction in the course of reading a treatise on welfare economics. In this attention, qualitative differences are fundamental.[30]

The world in which these characters move is itself a qualitatively rich world. It contains a "plain, bare, monotonous vault of a schoolroom," and it contains the flags and the "clashing and banging band" of the circus; it contains the "graceful equestrian Tyrolean flower-act," and it also contains a "river that ran purple with ill-smelling dye," not to mention "the piston of a steam engine . . . like the head of an elephant in a state of melancholy madness." This world thickly surrounds the characters, creating both opportunities and impediments. In the account of the daily activity of factory workers, we see vividly how circumstances that social choice can change affect not only utility but also the capacities for thought and selection, not only pleasure but also freedom.

The economic-utilitarian view of persons is that they are mere containers or sites of satisfaction. The novel, by contrast, sees the boundaries between one person and another as among the world's most salient facts. Factory worker Stephen Blackpool's fatigue and isolation are not mitigated in the least by the fact that Bounderby is well-fed and complacent; Louisa's misery at her marriage is not raised up by her father's contentment. Pain and happiness are shown as things that belong to separate individuals, who must bear them alone, and who have just one life in which to strive for happiness.

The ability of individuals to choose the shape of that life as separate centers of agency is itself given tremendous emphasis. In the many miseries of Stephen's life, none is greater than his inability to influence its course—his lack of access to the legal system, his lack of access to fair contractual dealings with his employers. The novel represents human beings as creatures for whom the freedom to choose is of profound and passionate importance, an importance not reducible to pleasure, but one that sets conditions within which any pleasure can be a truly human pleasure. In this way it shows us that the workers of Coketown do not suffer from economic deprivation alone; for even if well-fed and safe, they would be leading subhuman lives in respect of freedom. Indeed, the least fully human life in the novel is probably that of Mrs. Gradgrind, on account of the way she surrenders her boundaries and her agency to the forces that sustain her, however benignly.

We can notice, too, that, here and elsewhere, the novel takes it for granted that preferences are not given from outside the lives that the individuals manage to lead. Just as the workers set their sights low because they know only an impoverished life, so the preference of Mrs. Gradgrind for not being fully a person must be seen as a product of the crushing forces that have throughout life borne down upon her.

All these features, I would again argue, are elements of the genre, of the way in which it invites its readers to look at characters in their social setting and to wonder about their lives. So too, I would claim, is its complex behavioral theory, so different in its attributions of motives from the utilitarian theory of self-interested maximization. The characters of *Hard Times* all seek the satisfaction of their preferences in many ways; they also display sympathies and commitments that are not merely useful. The circus is a community built on the principle of mutual aid and mutual concern, in which individuals define their goals in terms of the happiness of others, frequently in ways that entail real sacrifice. But the novel's other characters are also circus people, at least in some part of their lives. Here again, we encounter an exception: just as Mrs. Gradgrind is at the limiting point of humanity with respect to agency, so Bitzer, monstrous product of the utilitarian system, is to altruism. He manipulates throughout the novel; even his self-conscious parroting of the sentiments of utilitarianism is his ghastly way of getting what he wants at his teacher's expense. He cannot understand what love and gratitude are; to him the heart is a useful pump, no more. But, as the novel shows us, Bitzer is chillingly weird and not quite human. From our first glimpse of his "cold eyes" and his skin, "so unwholesomely deficient in the natural tinge," we know that we are dealing with a monster. The monstrosity in Bitzer is his incapacity for any sympathy or commitment that extend beyond a use of others to serve his own ends. It is a feature of the genre, a feature of the way in which realist novels solicit and cultivate the imagination, that this figure repels our sympathy and our identification; even asking what it is like to be him is difficult, so alien is he made to seem.

If we want to consider one case in which all these differences between the novel and a Gradgrind-style utilitarian treatise can be summed up, we might focus on our relationship, as readers, to Mr. Gradgrind. If Mr. Gradgrind wrote an economics book, placing himself in it as a character in a way consistent with his system, what would be interesting and salient about the Gradgrind character? How would it address the reader's imagination? Only, clearly, through the fact that his life was governed by the laws that govern lives in the aggregate, and through the fact that he exemplifies the so-called rationality of the economic bargainer. Only under these descriptions could Mr. Gradgrind appear in his own book. The "story" of such a book would be the story of transactions; and its reader would be held to it not by love or fear, but by a mixture of intellectual exhilaration and rational self-interest. Such is the moral content of the Gradgrind genre, if genre it is.

How different our own relation to Mr. Gradgrind. What is it, in fact, that makes Mr. Gradgrind an interesting character for the reader, a gripping and ultimately a deeply moving character, in a way that Bitzer and Bounderby are not? It is, surely, his failure to be the sort of person his utilitarian theory represents. Bitzer is just weird; we cannot identify with him or wonder about him, for we sense that all within is empty. A novel peopled entirely by Bitzers would be a kind of science fiction and would not grip its reader in the manner characteristic of the traditional novel, which relies on bonds of identification and sympathy. But we do, by contrast, find ourselves taking a sympathetic interest in Mr. Gradgrind; we are encouraged to wonder about him even as we criticize him, to care about what befalls him—in short, to experience him as an interesting and significant character in a compelling novel. Built into our aesthetic experience is a certain shaping of desire.

What in Mr. Gradgrind arouses this desire? It is, we have to say, the fact that we know early on that he is not like his own theoretical constructs—that he is qualitatively distinct and separate in a way not recognized in his theory's vision of persons, that he is motivated by love, commitment, and plain decency in ways that do not find expression in his theory of human action. We notice how he refuses to endorse Bounderby's rude dismissal of Sissy's father. We are aware of high-minded humanitarian motives in his preference for reason over fancy, motives which may have been misdirected but which are admirable in themselves. Above all, we notice a degree of love for his daughter, a hesitation in his implementation of his schemes for her, that makes us think, So this man has a soul. This vision of Gradgrind as a complex agent, this respect before a soul, is built into the genre itself, into its modes of address to its reader. Without a certain number of characters to whom we can have this relation, we lose interest, and our novel-reading pleasure ceases. But when we engage in such relations we are seeing the world from a point of view very unlike that recommended by Gradgrind economics.

This novel tells a story. In so doing, it gets its readers involved with the characters, caring about their projects, their hopes and fears, participating in their attempts to unravel the mysteries and perplexities of their lives. The participation of the reader is made explicit at many points in the narration. And it is brought home to readers that the story is in certain ways their own story, showing possibilities for human life and choice that are in certain respects their own to seize, though their concrete circumstances may differ greatly. Thus their attempts to interpret and evaluate are encouraged to be both affectionate and critical: for the text portrays them as social agents responsible for making a world that is either like or unlike the world within its pages, agents who must in life stand in some emotional and practical relation to the problems of the working classes and to the conduct of managers and leaders. In imagining things that do not really exist, the novel, by its own account, is not being "idle": for it is helping its readers to acknowledge their own world and to choose more reflectively in it.

In short, the experience of reading this novel has, not surprisingly, just the properties that it imputes to the experience of novel-reading, when (through the puzzled eyes of Mr. Gradgrind) it describes the tendency of the people of Coketown to prefer novel-reading to the reading of government statistics: "They wondered about human nature, human passions, human hopes and fears, the struggles, triumphs and defeats, the cares and joys and sorrows, the lives and deaths, of common men and women! They sometimes, after fifteen hours' work, sat down to read mere fables about men and women, more or less like themselves, and about children, more or less like their own. They took De Foe to their bosoms, instead of Euclid,and seemed to be on the whole more comforted by Goldsmith than by Cocker." As Mr. Gradgrind wonders about "this unaccountable fact," we of course notice that our own preferences and current activity are being described.

So far we have spoken of features of the novel that it shares with numerous narrative genres: its commitment to the separateness of persons and to the irreducibility of quality to quantity; its sense that what happens to individuals in the world has enormous importance; its commitment to describe the events of life not from an external perspective of detachment, as the doings and movings of ants or machine parts, but from within, as invested with the complex significances with which human beings invest their own lives. The novel has an even greater commitment to the richness of the inner world than do many other narrative genres, and a greater commitment to the moral relevance of following a life through all of its adventures in all of its concrete context. To this extent, it is even more profoundly opposed than other genres to the reductive economic way of seeing the world, more committed to qualitative distinctions.

But with Mr. Gradgrind's musings about the strange library habits of the Coketown working classes, we come upon an especially distinctive feature of the genre: namely, its interest in the ordinary, in the daily lives and struggles of ordinary men and women. In entering the homes of factory workers as involved friends, the reader investigates and embraces their lives. This means that the reader has already the moral experience that Louisa is represented as having when she visits the home of Stephen Blackpool and is jolted out of all calculation by the perception that a "Hand" has a name, a face, a daily life, a complex soul, a history:

> For the first time in her life, Louisa had come into one of the dwellings of the Coketown Hands; for the first time in her life, she was face to face with

anything like individuality in connexion with them. She knew of their existence by hundreds and by thousands. She knew what results in work a given
number of them would produce in a given space of time. She knew them
in crowds passing to and from their nests, like ants or beetles. But she knew
from her reading infinitely more of the ways of toiling insects than of these
toiling men and women.

This is one of the most striking of many self-referential passages in the novel.
Coming well after much of the novel's own detailed description of the life of
Stephen Blackpool, it reminds us that our own education and experience as
readers have been and are very different from the economic education of
the young Gradgrinds. The person brought up solely on economic texts has
not been encouraged to think of workers (or, indeed, anyone else) as fully
human beings, with stories of their own to tell.

This is not altogether an antiutilitarian point, for one might with justice
observe that the knowledge that each citizen has a complex history and a
story of his or her own to tell is one good way of elaborating the core of
Bentham's idea that each person is to count as one and none as more than
one. Here, then, as with the significance of pain, as with the central importance of altruism, the novel suggests a subtle internal critique of certain species of utilitarianism, not its complete repudiation. The suggestion is that
what is finest in the theory has not been well served by the theory in its full
elaboration (especially, though not only, in contemporary economics); that
a different and fuller vision of persons is necessary to do justice to the deepest insights of Benthamism itself.

The novel's depiction of working-class life has some grave flaws. There is
some sentimentality. There is an odd failure in basic literary technique, in
that the mysterious promise of Stephen to Rachel, which prevents him from
joining the union, is never explained at all—and yet it is permitted to determine the shape of the plot. Again, Dickens is so suspicious of all collective
action that the work of trade unions is portrayed in a light manifestly unfair,
even by the standards of his own nonfictional writing of this period.[31] In
general, we have many reasons to sympathize with George Orwell's criticism of Dickens: in his commitment to the individual, Dickens fails to concern himself sufficiently with possibilities for political action and institutional change; and because he fails to imagine such changes, he is too easily
satisfied with the prospect of giving the poor a little relief and leisure time.[32]

Nonetheless, his novel presents a political vision that is not undermined by these defects in its explicit political recommendations. The essential point made in the Louisa/Stephen passage stands: reading a novel like this one makes us acknowledge the equal humanity of members of social classes other than our own, makes us acknowledge workers as deliberating subjects with complex loves and aspirations and a rich inner world. It makes us see their poverty and their oppressive labor conditions in relation to those emotions and aspirations. Its insistence on the complexity of the lives of individuals and the salience of individual differences discourages simple utopian political solutions and suggests an approach that both focuses on freedom and leaves much room for diversity.[33] But it is well aware that freedom has material conditions and can be strangled by material inequality. In its insistent focus on these facts, it inspires compassion and the passion for justice.[34]

If, then, from Gradgrind's viewpoint novels are bad economics, lacking in mathematical refinement, from the novel's viewpoint sophisticated economics of the Gradgrind sort is a bad novel—crude in its powers of representation and depiction, falsely detached from the situations of fellow human beings, impoverished in the range of sentiments it recognizes and inspires. Consider, too, the stories its utilitarian characters tell about themselves, and what clumsy fictions these are: for example, Gradgrind's plotless account of his victory over Joseph and George and the other imaginary Gradgrinds, the "leaden little books'" account of the "good grown-up baby [who] invariably got to the Savings-bank, and the bad grown-up baby [who] invariably got transported." The failures of the Gradgrind imagination can hardly, the novel claims, be politically irrelevant, for what one can do to ants and beetles is, morally, altogether different from what one can do to a being whom one sees as invested with the dignity and mystery of humanness. The social atrocities practiced in the factory—the long monotonous working hours, the unhealthy and unsafe working conditions—are not unconnected with the vision of the "Hands" nourished by utilitarian education, according to which they are, in fact, just bodily parts and nothing more, producing hands and consuming stomachs. Dehumanize the worker in thought, and it is far easier to deny him or her the respect that human life calls forth.

The first principle of the science of economics, according to Sissy Jupe, miserably failing at her lesson, is "to do unto others as I would that they should do unto me." (To which Mr. Gradgrind observes, "shaking his head, that all this was very bad; that it showed the necessity of infinite grinding at the mill of knowledge, as per system, schedule, blue book, report, and tabular statements A to Z.")[35] I am claiming that Sissy Jupe's first principle is not merely represented in this novel; it is built into the novel's entire structure as its guiding principle, for we are invited to concern ourselves with the fates of others like ourselves, attaching ourselves to them both by sympathetic friendship and by empathetic identification. When, then, we are invited at the close to think what we shall do, our natural response will be, if we have read with attention and concern, to do unto other ordinary men and women as to ourselves, viewing the poorest as one who we might be, and seeing in the most ordinary and even squalid circumstances a place where we have made in fancy our dwelling.[36]

This brings me to one further feature of the novel: its capacity to give pleasure. Its moral operations are not independent of its aesthetic excellence. It binds us to the workers because it causes us to take pleasure in their company. A tedious novel would not have had the same moral power, or rather, the precision of attention that makes for interest is itself a moral feature. This is no incidental aspect of *Hard Times*, but one that it prominently stresses. The moral antitype of Gradgrind's school is Sleary's circus, whose capacity to please is closely linked to its moral superiority. And if we ask once again our obvious question about differences between this work and a text in Gradgrind political economy, we surely must answer that one of the greatest is that this book is fun to read. Like the circus, it contains humor and adventure, grotesqueness and surprise, music (note the frequent use of musical metaphors), rhythm, and motion. Its language is lyrical and full of poetic figures. Its plot is dramatically compelling; its characters inspire our trust and sympathy, or excite our laughter, or frighten us, or generate anger and disdain—or some complex combination of several of these. Its pleasure is more complexly critical, more richly moral, than the pleasure of the circus; it depicts the circus as intellectually incomplete, insisting on a complex mixture of storytelling and social criticism that the novel as a genre is well equipped to offer. But in all of its art, the novel self-referentially acknowledges the moral importance of the play of the imagination. As Sleary twice observes, "People mutht be amuthed." The capacity of this novel to play, to give delight—a capacity inseparable, as in the circus, from the craft that informs it—is part of what makes it valuable to human life.[37] Unlike Louisa, the reader of this novel "com[es] upon Reason through the tender light of Fancy." We must now ask why this should be thought to be important.

Fancy and Wonder

I have spoken of the novel, of this novel, as embodying in its form a certain sort of moral/political vision—democratic, compassionate, committed to complexity, choice, and qualitative differences. I have said that it does not merely represent a competition between fancy and political economy, but also enacts it in its structure, in its ways of conversing with its hypothetical reader. Now, however, we must go deeper, trying to say more about the fiction-making imagination, about "fancy" itself, as the novel represents it. For it is this activity of the mind that the Gradgrind school above all abhors and seeks to extirpate; it is this capacity that the novel most centrally defends as necessary for a good life, and that it triumphantly, exuberantly exemplifies in its every chapter.

Fancy is the novel's name for the ability to see one thing as another, to see one thing in another. We might therefore also call it the metaphorical imagination. It begins simply, as an almost instinctual reflex of mind (only Bitzer and Mrs. Gradgrind lack it totally). Even Louisa, forbidden its cultivation, sees shapes in the fire, endows perceived patterns with a significance that is not present in the bare sense perception itself.[38] Things look like other things, or more precisely, the other things are seen in the immediate things, as Louisa is aware at one and the same time both of the conjured images and of the fact that they are not present realities.[39] (With the good sense natural to fancy, she does not rush into the fire to grasp the images she reads there—a good sense, we might add, that eludes her father, who objects to a flower pattern in a carpet on the grounds that one does not tramp on flowers with one's boots. Sissy, objecting, knows that the flowers, being flowers of the fancy, will not be hurt by the boots of reality.) Seeing a perception, then, as pointing to something beyond itself, seeing in the things that are perceptible and at hand other things that are not before one's eyes—this is fancy, and this is why Mr. Gradgrind disapproves of it. In childhood, the novel reminds us, this ability is usually cultivated in countless ways—by games, stories, nursery rhymes—all of which are forbidden in the Gradgrind scheme for education:

No little Gradgrind had ever seen a face in the moon. . . . No little Gradgrind had ever learnt the silly jingle "Twinkle, twinkle, little star; how I
wonder what you are!" No little Gradgrind had ever known wonder on the
subject, each little Gradgrind having at five years old dissected the Great
Bear like a Professor Owen, and driven Charles's Wain like a locomotive
engine driver. No little Gradgrind had ever associated a cow in a field with
that famous cow with the crumpled horn who tossed the dog who worried
the cat who killed the rat who ate the malt, or with that yet more famous
cow who swallowed Tom Thumb: it had never heard of those celebrities,
and had only been introduced to a cow as a gramnivorous ruminating
quadruped with several stomachs.

From the Gradgrind viewpoint, this is the omission of useless frills, leaving
more time for the real stuff of education. But the novel announces, and
shows, that it is the omission of a morally crucial ability, without which both
personal and social relations are impoverished.

As Louisa, chastened and empty, returns home, the authorial voice reminds the reader of the difference between her memories of home and the
influences that home and the childlike imagination usually exert:

Neither, as she approached her old home now, did any of the best influences
of old home descend upon her. The dreams of childhood—its airy fables;
its graceful, beautiful, humane, impossible adornments of the world beyond: so good to be believed in once, so good to be remembered when
outgrown, for then the least among them rises to the stature of a great
Charity in the heart, suffering little children, to come into the midst of it,
and to keep with their pure hands a garden in the stony ways of this
world . . . —what had she to do with these? Remembrances of how she had
journeyed to the little that she knew, by the enchanted roads of what she
and millions of innocent creatures had hoped and imagined; of how, first
coming upon Reason through the tender light of Fancy, she had seen it a
beneficent god, deferring to gods as great as itself: not a grim idol, cruel
and cold, with its victims bound hand to foot, and its big dumb shape set up
with a sightless stare, never to be moved by anything but so many calculated
tons of leverage—what had she to do with these?

Here the novel makes some complicated connections. How exactly is fancy
connected with charity and generosity, with general human sympathy and
a beneficent use of reason?

The man in the moon, the cow with the crumpled horn, the little star—
in all these cases the child fancies that a form, which perception presents as
a simple physical object, has a complex inner life, in some ways mysterious,
in some ways like the child's own. To see moon craters as a face, to speak to
a star, to tell a story about a cow—these are things that the factual detached
imagination of economic science is unwilling to do. But there is, as the novel
says, a charity in this willingness to go beyond the evidence, and this charity
is a preparation for greater charities in life.

Consider, now, what it is to see a human being. Perception represents a
physical object, possibly in motion. It has a certain shape, rather like the
one we ascribe to ourselves. Well, how do we really know what sort of physical object this is and how to behave toward it? Do we ever have unimpeach-
able evidence that it is not a sophisticated robot or automaton? That it does
indeed have an inner world of the sort that novels depict? How do we know,
really, that this is a face before us and not, say, a complex mechanical object,
a fiendishly clever machine? Where could such evidence ever be obtained?
In this sense, Dickens suggests, all of human life is a going beyond the facts,
an acceptance of generous fancies, a projection of our own sentiments and
inner activities onto the forms we perceive about us (and a reception from
this interaction of images of ourselves, our own inner world). We are all of
us, insofar as we interact morally and politically, fanciful projectors, makers
of and believers in fictions and metaphors.[40] The point, then, is that the
"fact" school, which denies subjective experience to cows and horses, humanity to workers, engages in fiction making as much as do novel-readers
and fanciers. Its adamant denials of life and humanity go, like the others'
assertions, beyond the limits of the evidence. We never know for sure the
contents of this perceived shape's heart; we have a choice only between a
generous construction and a mean-spirited construction.[41] Seeing-in, or
fancy, the great charity in the heart, nourishes a generous construal of the
world. This construal is not only, as the novel suggests, more adequate as an
explanation of the totality of human behavior as we experience it, but also
a cause of better ways of living.[42]

In my law school class, when we reached this point in the novel, before I
made any observations of my own about fancy, I decided to ask my students
about nursery rhymes: why did Dickens attach so much importance to
them? I called on a dark-haired student in the second row who had said

little in the class so far, though what he had said was especially thoughtful. Mr. Riley, I said, did you ever sing "Twinkle, twinkle little star"? Yes, Mr. Riley had. What did you think about when you sang that song? Do you remember how it made you feel? (Asking such questions in the University of Chicago Law School might be thought to be as odd as bringing Sleary's circus into the the the Gradgrind schoolroom.) Slowly and quietly, in a flat Kansas voice, Mr. Riley began to describe—with a Dickensian poetry I cannot recapture—the image he used to see of a sky beautifully blazing with stars and bands of bright color. This wonderful sight somehow, he said, led him to look in a new way at his cocker spaniel. He would look into the dog's eyes and wonder what the dog was really feeling and thinking, and whether it might be feeling sadness. Now it seemed to him that it was right to wonder about the dog's experience, and to think of the dog as having both love for him and the capacity to feel pleasure and pain. Sitting there in his T-shirt in the second row, Mr. Riley described the eyes of his dog with a grace and artistry that brought a hush to the lecture hall. There was no sentimentality in the description, difficult though it is to recapture it without giving the impression that there was. All this, in turn, he said, led to new ways of thinking about his parents and about other children.

Why did Mr. Riley think that the starry sky was benign and not malevolent? Why did it lead him to attribute love and goodness to his cocker spaniel, rather than devilishness and sadism? Why did it lead him to wonder compassionately about the dog's sadness, rather than to take pleasure in the animal's pain? Mr. Riley felt that this could not be fully explained; I am sure its explanation has much to do with Mr. Riley's parents and a feeling of love and safety he was beginning to derive from the context in which he heard the song. But the fact is that the nursery song itself, like other such songs, nourishes the ascription of humanity, and the prospect of friendship, rather than paranoid sentiments of being persecuted by a hateful being in the sky. It tells the child to regard the star as "like a diamond," not like a missile of destruction, and also not like a machine good only for production and consumption. In this sense, the birth of fancy is non-neutral and does, as Dickens indicates, nourish a generous construction of the seen. Mr. Riley, with Dickens, was claiming that this makes a difference in the moral life.[43]

We see the difference in the novel, for example, in the contrasting ways of regarding workers: Bounderby seeing only self-interest, the novel seeing a tangled variety of motives. We see it in the ways of contemplating possibilities for political change—for even when the ways of the world are "stony," fancy can imagine a garden growing there. We see it, too, in the contrasting attitudes of the circus and of Tom Gradgrind toward the appetites of the body. The circus people are passionate in a romantic and tender manner, always seeing in one another a complex life, and delighting in that. Of Tom, the novel remarks, with heavy irony, "It was altogether unaccountable that a young gentleman whose imagination had been strangled in his cradle, should be still inconvenienced by its ghost in the form of grovelling sensualities." Seeing bodies only as physical objects in motion produces an impoverished sexual life. It is indeed this very thought that is at the root of the feminist critique of "objectification," the tendency to see one's sexual partner as thinglike, therefore lacking in particularity and autonomy.

It is by no means accidental, then, that the utilitarians are depicted throughout with language at once phallic and military, as aggressive weapons conducting a remorseless assault on all that is sensuous, playful, and in the manner of the circus, musical. Mr. Gradgrind is a "cannon loaded to the muzzle with facts," a "galvanizing apparatus," directed against "the tender young imaginations that were to be stormed away." By contrast, the approach of fancy is depicted as musical and sensuous, as delighting in the dexterity of speech and gesture, the intricate rhythm and texture of words themselves. Gradgrind language sounds hard, intrusive, its cadences fierce and abrupt. As language, its body moves itself with a pitiless directness, combining aggressiveness with self-righteous complacency: "The M'Choakumchild school was all fact, and the school of design was all fact, and the relations between master and man were all fact, and everything was fact between the lying-in hospital and the cemetery, and what you couldn't state in figures, or show to be purchasable in the cheapest market and saleable in the dearest, was not, and never should be, world without end. Amen." By contrast, the speech of fancy has, so to speak, a flexible and acrobatic circus body, a surprising exuberant variety. It loves the physical texture of language and plays with it, teasing and caressing the reader. Even when it speaks about its adversaries, it cannot long restrain itself from treating them as partners in a game of words, in which delight is taken for its own sake. Thus the many alliterative linguistic games in the depiction of the Gradgrind house, where the narrator enjoys the play of his supple speech around their blunter bodies—as in this passage, where an initially straightforward description becomes more and more joyously sensuous, until the play of the tongue quite takes over, defeating its own subject matter:

> The little Gradgrinds had cabinets in various departments of science too. They had a little conchological cabinet, and a little metallurgical cabinet, and a little mineralogical cabinet; and the specimens were all arranged and labelled, and the bits of stone and ore looked as though they might have been broken from the parent substances by those tremendously hard instruments their own names; and, to paraphrase the idle legend of Peter Piper, who had never found his way into their nursery, If the greedy little Gradgrinds grasped at more than this, what was it for good gracious goodness sake, that the greedy little Gradgrinds grasped at!

Here the literary imagination opposes to the dull instruments of the names used by economics its own very different language, and is carried away by playfulness. It thus deliberately embodies and evokes forms of desire and sensuality profoundly opposed to those it imputes to Gradgrind's version of economics. Imagine language as a way of touching a human body, Dickens suggests, and you have a way of scrutinizing the claims of Gradgrind's theory to stand for us in the fullness of our selves.

I might add here that Dickens has sometimes been represented as repressing sexuality, especially female sexuality. I believe that this judgment, though it certainly derives support from his treatment of many female characters, neglects evidence on the other side—in particular, this novel's depiction of the ways in which tongue and mind approach a human form. It is not only that a crude aggressiveness is condemned while a more varied, and more playful, sexuality is celebrated; it is also plain that this sensuous play is linked repeatedly with the influence of the female—and both with the interest of the circus in music and narrative art. The susceptible, playful side of life, the side lost, David Copperfield says, by most adult males, is the side out of which novels are generated.[44] This one is no exception, clearly. In the circus, men and women are equal: "All the fathers could dance upon rolling casks, . . . ride upon anything, jump over everything. . . . All the mothers could (and did) dance . . . and perform rapid acts on barebacked steeds; none of them were at all particular in respect of showing their legs." In place of the rather sexless ingenues who inhabit so much of Dickens's middle-class world, the circus puts the estimable Josephine, who made a will at age twelve "expressive of her dying desire to be drawn to the grave by the two piebald ponies."

With this mention of play, we come to a further element in fancy, which we must now explore to complete our account of its social role. When a child learns to fancy, it is learning something useless. This is the Gradgrind school's main objection to it: storybooks are "idle." Facts are what we need, "the one thing needful," and what use has anyone ever gotten from the man in the moon? But the child who takes delight in stories and nursery rhymes is getting the idea that not everything in human life has a use. It is learning a mode of engagement with the world that does not focus exclusively on the idea of use, but is capable, too, of cherishing things for their own sake. And this the child takes into its relations with other human beings. It is not only the ability to endow a form with life that makes the metaphorical imagination morally valuable; it is the ability to view what one has constructed in fancy as serving no end beyond itself, as good and delightful for itself alone. Play and amusement are thus not simply adjuncts or supplements to human life, but are exemplary in a crucial way about how to view life's central elements. In this sense, the reader's delight in this novel has yet a further moral dimension as a preparation for moral activities of many kinds in life.

I can perhaps sum all this up by examining the two contrasting scenes of education presented in the Whitman extract that serves as one epigraph for this book and the passage from *Hard Times* with which I opened this chapter. Both are scenes in which a request for a definition or account of something has been made.

Bitzer has never loved a horse and obviously has no interest in thinking what it might be like to be one. With an air of finality and certainty, he recites the detached external description. The horse emerges as a useful machine, no more. How different is Whitman's speaker. First of all, he is motivated not by a mechanical urge to complete enumeration, but by the child's real curiosity, and by the sight and touch of the grass of which, lying in the grass, he speaks. His first response is to acknowledge that he does not finally know—to acknowledge, that is, a mystery in nature. All his ensuing answers are presented as guesses. He speaks first of his inner life, his hope; next, whimsically and not at all dogmatically, of a child's idea of God; then he tells the child that the grass is sort of like him, a young bit of vegetation—

he asks the child to see it as like himself. He then shows the child that it can have, as well, a social significance: one can see in it the equal vitality and dignity of all Americans, their equal rights and privileges across racial and ethnic differences. Then, turning in, we imagine, on himself, the speaker sees in the grass a darker set of significances, pondering in and through it the beauty of dead men. He endows even their corpses beneath the earth with beauty, speaking of them with a profoundly erotic reverence and tenderness—but in a way that does not exclude further thoughts of the grass as from elderly parents or prematurely dead children. And yet, in its darkness—too dark to come from old mothers or even from the mouths of those he has or might have loved—he sees an image of his own death.

Here we see all the abilities of fancy, deftly woven together: its ability to endow a perceived form with rich and complex significance; its generous construction of the seen; its preference for wonder over pat solutions; its playful and surprising movements, delightful for their own sake; its tenderness, its eroticism, its awe before the fact of human mortality. It is Dickens's view, as it is also Whitman's, that this imagination—including its playfulness, including its eroticism—is the necessary basis for good government of a country of equal and free citizens. With it, reason is beneficent, steered by a generous view of its objects; without its charity, reason is cold and cruel.[45]

We can now understand that the persistent exuberant metaphoricity of the language of *Hard Times* is no mere game, no stylistic diversion; it goes to the heart of the novel's moral theme. Even while the novel portrays the Gradgrind schoolroom, it cannot help comparing one thing to another, seeing one thing in another: two dark caves, in Mr. Gradgrind's eyes; a plantation of firs in his hair; the crust of a plum pie in the bald surface of the top of M'choakumchild's head. Even while it depicts the monotony and soul-crushing dreariness of the Coketown factory, it triumphs over it in language, comparing the coils of steam to serpents, the moving machine parts to "melancholy-mad elephants"—showing in these ways the human meaning of the inhuman. The novel cannot describe its opposition without doing battle with it, approaching it through Fancy and playfully surmounting it.[46]

The novel calls on us to interpret metaphors. But we can now say more: the novel presents *itself* as a metaphor. See the world in this way, and not in that, it suggests. Look at things as if they were like this story, and not in other ways recommended by social science. By reading the novel, we get not just a concrete set of images in terms of which to imagine this particular world, but also, and more significantly, a general cast of mind with which to approach our own.

I must now insist again that in this novel—and in my own view—there is no disparagement of reason or of the scientific search for truth. What I am criticizing is a particular scientific approach that claims to stand for truth and for reason. What I am saying about it is that it fails to stand for truth insofar as it dogmatically misrepresents the complexity of human beings and human life. It fails to stand for reason when it uncritically trusts half-baked perceptions and crude psychological theories. The novel speaks not of dismissing reason, but of coming upon it in a way illuminated by fancy, which is here seen as a faculty at once creative and veridical. The alternative I am proposing is not Sleary's circus. The circus offers the reader essential metaphors of art, discipline, play, and love; but even within the novel its attitudes are shown as politically incomplete, too ill-educated and whimsical to govern a nation. The novel indicates that political and economic treatises of an abstract and mathematical sort would be perfectly consistent with its purpose—so long as the view of the human being underlying the treatises was the richer view available in the novel; so long as they do not lose sight of what they are, for efficiency, omitting. Government cannot investigate the life story of every citizen in the way a novel does with its characters; it can, however, know that each citizen has a complex history of this sort, and it can remain aware that the norm in principle would be to acknowledge the separateness, freedom, and qualitative difference of each in the manner of the novel. I shall shortly give an example of a scientific economic approach based on this more complete information.

In fact, it is clear that the abilities displayed and cultivated in the novel are incomplete without both an economics and a moral/political theory— although it is also the case that abstract theory is likely to prove blind and motivationally impotent without the cultivation of these abilities. The experience of reading the novel implicitly involves reflection about what human activities are the most important, and how political action of various sorts does or does not support those activities. This means that the novel invites us to reflect critically: has the novel been correct in identifying those activities and the conditions needed for their realization? The description of the Coketown library speaks of "human nature, human passions, human hopes and fears," as the subject matter of the novel. In so doing, it reminds us that the novel does not purchase its attention to social context and to individual variety at the price of jettisoning moral and political theory. It forges a complex relationship with its reader in which, on the one hand, the reader is urged to care about specific features of circumstance and history and to see these as relevant for social choice, but on the other hand, is reminded always to recognize that human beings in different spheres do have common passions, hopes, and fears—the need to confront death, the desire for learning, the deep bonds of the family.[47] To see that is already to engage in theoretical reflection. This reflection is solicited by the genre itself, as *Hard Times* correctly states, and it invites criticism and completion from philosophical theories of a more formal sort. The novel's insights commend themselves as relatively reliable from the fact that they elicit deep responses across boundaries of place and time. On the other hand, they can go wrong and need theoretical corroboration. The novel itself imposes some constraints: its insights are incompatible with many political theories, leading in the direction of a liberal theory of the Kantian or Aristotelian sort, in which separateness, freedom, and a complex account of human flourishing will all play a role. But the precise specification of the theory and its conception of flourishing remains a matter for further philosophical argument.

In its engagement with a general notion of the human being, this novel (like many novels) is, I think, while particularistic, not relativistic. That is, it recognizes human needs that transcend boundaries of time, place, class, religion, and ethnicity, and it makes the focus of its moral deliberation the question of their adequate fulfillment. Its criticism of concrete political and social situations relies on a notion of what it is for a human being to flourish, and this notion itself, while extremely general and in need of further specification, is neither local nor sectarian. On the other hand, part of the idea of flourishing is a deep respect for qualitative difference—so the norm enjoins that governments, wherever they are, should attend to citizens in all their concreteness and variety, responding in a sensitive way to historical and personal contingencies. But that is itself a universal injunction and part of a universal picture of humanness. And it is by relying on this universal ideal that the novel, so different from a guidebook or even an anthropological field report, makes readers participants in the lives of people very different from themselves and also critics of the class distinctions that give people similarly constructed an unequal access to flourishing. Once again, these insights need corroboration from theoretical arguments; they are not complete in themselves. But the novel as a genre, in its basic structure and aspiration, is, I think, a defender of the Enlightenment ideal of the equality and dignity of all human life, not of uncritical traditionalism. It is opposed to the perversion of that ideal in the name of a pseudoscientific approach in economics, and also to its insensitive application with insufficient respect for stories told within a concrete historical context—not to the ideal itself.

The utilitarian economist will now make three replies. The first (and strongest) reply is that the utilitarian theory—at least in its contemporary economic form—is not intended to offer a complete account of every aspect of people and their inner worlds. It is intended to enable us to make predictions, and it may serve that function well even when it does not get the phenomenological story right. Sometimes it may serve that function better by not getting the inner story right in all its complexity: for good models frequently have to be simpler than reality. In that sense, rational-choice models should be seen, not as competitors to the insights of the novel, but as pursuing a different project.

This reply seems plausible enough, within limits. There should be in principle no objection to the adoption of simplified models for predictive purposes. So long as they serve that use well and are not called on for other purposes, the novel-reader should not object. That they do serve these predictive purposes well when they diverge greatly from the ways in which people actually think and choose remains at present uncertain. Most uses of economics to analyze nonmarket behavior make their predictions retrospectively, arguing that the theory *would have* predicted an actual result; there is obviously much room for ad hoc maneuvering in this procedure, especially given the elusiveness of the concept of utility. Examples of testable before-the-fact predictions are too few for us to be certain that these techniques really have a superior predictive power, and there have been numerous challenges even to the retrospective predictions that have been offered.[48] Certainly, however, the novel-reader should not object to the testing of such approaches to determine to what extent they do have predictive advantages over more complicated approaches.

On the other hand, novel-readers should point out that this makes their own function more important, not less. When simplified conceptions of the human being are in widespread use for predictive purposes, it is all the more important to keep reminding ourselves of the richer picture of human life to which such simplified models are ultimately accountable. As the novel suggests, seeing people in the way recommended by economics does tend to spill over into the conduct of life and the choice of policies: Gradgrind's vision of the world is in that sense not an innocent "as if" operation, but a way of restructuring the human world that has, if thoroughly and habitually carried out, profound significance for the shape of human societies.[49] If we use it for its usefulness, we should make sure that we master it and that it does not master us. We should not forget that some of its proponents do claim that economics gives a complete account of human deliberative activity—that, as George Stigler put it, "all of man's deliberative, forward-looking behavior follows the principles of economics."[50] We should be on our guard against the ease with which simplified models tend to take over and begin to look like the whole of reality. We should resist that tendency. To that end, we should insist all the more on novel-reading, a vivid reminder of a human sense of value and an exercise of the valuational abilities that make us fully human.

We can add, furthermore, that it is not as if we have to make a choice between the utilitarian vision and a collapse into mere sentiment without science, for the novel itself makes its contribution to economic science, as we shall shortly see, and the economist should take very seriously the contention that a more complicated theory of the person might deliver better predictions. Many contemporary projects in economics, and even in law-and-economics, are making use of these more complicated notions of the person, precisely for predictive reasons.

Returning to a point mentioned at the beginning of this chapter, we now need to recall that there are actually two types of utilitarian predictive theory, which differ in their relationship to intuitions and in their capacity for making testable predictions. The type of utilitarian view that takes actual behavior as criterial of agents' preferences ("revealed-preference" theory) seems capable of adapting itself very flexibly to empirical facts; on the other hand, its predictions are bound to be vague and virtually impossible to test scientifically, since no definite account is given of the utility that a rational agent is maximizing. Without some account of what lies behind choices, we cannot get enough of a handle on what people value in order to make predictions of what they will choose in a new instance. Choices are highly contextual, and for this reason choices in a present context are poor predictors of future behavior.[51]

By contrast, the brand of economic utilitarianism that does give some definite account of utility (the type preferred by Becker and Posner) does deliver definite and testable predictions. But it is here that we need to remain aware of the difference between that utilitarian account of what individuals value and the richer account available in our literary (and our everyday) experience. Perhaps the differences will not matter for predictive purposes—although since they are considerable it would be a bit surprising if they did not. In any case, it is precisely when we choose to use such models for the sake of simplicity that we should remind ourselves of a richer picture of human action.

The economist's second, related, complaint is that I have treated utilitarian theory as both descriptive and normative, whereas it claims only to be a descriptive theory. In that sense, once again, it need not be in competition with the novel, insofar as the latter offers readers an ethical norm and cultivates sympathetic emotions related to that norm. Once again, the novel-reader will reply, for "rationality," as used in economics, is both a descriptive and a subtly normative and evaluative term. It is contrasted with mere sentiment and irrational emotion; it connotes good sense rather than silliness. In Posner's writing on justice, to cite just one example, it is used to castigate the U.S. Supreme Court for making privacy decisions that do not conform to what the economic model would recommend.[52] Mr. Gradgrind is, once again, not a straw man, for in his dismissal of fancy and emotion in favor of his own narrow conception of the facts, he stands for a normative distinction that the economic profession does indeed make, and for which it can justly be criticized. One can see the normative self-understanding of the theory particularly clearly in development economics, where its models are taken to yield information that should provide a sufficient basis for normative policy-making; I shall shortly argue that this has pernicious results.

Finally, the economist will insist that the utility-based model can in fact accommodate all of the novelist's insights, since all the information about human deliberation and value discussed here can simply be assigned the appropriate weightings and put into rational-choice preference-based calculations. Novel-readers will doubt, first of all, that this is a mere trivial modification—for they have argued that the model itself has substantive commitments of its own that are in some respects at odds with those they defend. But they will also observe that, to the extent that this is the economist's reply, the economist appears to be conceding that his theory does not, after all, offer an account of *rationality*. Such a theory would certainly have to include an account of how people assign the weights they do to different options in their deliberations, and which such deliberations are well done. All this work has to be done first by deliberation, before "rationality" in this thin economic sense even gets going.[53]

Sissy Jupe's Economics Lesson

What does all of this mean for economics and its political implications?[54] The public role of economics in measuring the quality of life is in fact the topic of Sissy Jupe's first lesson in the subject. Our interest in Dickens's novel should be increased by the fact that it corresponds still, even in its broad satirical elements, to much of the practice of development economics, and to public policy as influenced by it.

This is how the Gradgrind school, then as now, proceeds (Sissy narrating to Louisa):

> "And he said, Now, this schoolroom is a nation. And in this nation, there are fifty millions of money. Isn't this a prosperous nation? Girl number twenty, isn't this a prosperous nation, and a'n't you in a thriving state?"
>
> "What did you say?" asked Louisa.
>
> "Miss Louisa, I said I didn't know. I thought I couldn't know whether it was a prosperous nation or not, and whether I was in a thriving state or not, unless I knew who had got the Money and whether any of it was mine. But that had nothing to do with it. It was not in the figures at all," said Sissy, wiping her eyes.
>
> "That was a great mistake of yours," observed Louisa.

Today in fact, when the prosperity of nations is compared in "tabular form," by far the most common strategy is simply to enumerate GNP per capita.[55] This crude measure, of course, as Sissy immediately recognizes, does not even tell us about the distribution of wealth and income and thus can give high marks to nations with large inequalities. But avoiding the inequality and consequent misery depicted in *Hard Times* might seem to be a very important part of the quality of life in a nation. Furthermore, such an approach, focusing exclusively on the monetary, fails to tell us about how the human beings who have or do not have the money are functioning with respect to various significant activities that are not well correlated with GNP. It does not even tell us about life expectancy and infant mortality—let alone health, education, political rights, the quality of ethnic and racial and gender relations.

A slightly more sophisticated approach measures, as Gradgrind would wish, the total or average utility of the population, amalgamating satisfactions. This is, of course, the utilitarian approach that has been my focus throughout, as it is the novel's. This approach at least has the advantage of looking at how resources work for people, in promoting human aims of various sorts. But it has disadvantages that the novel makes all too plain. In addition to ignoring personal separateness in the way I have discussed, and using an extremely crude view of persons as containers of satisfaction, it ignores the fact that desires and satisfactions are highly malleable, and that people who are especially miserable can adapt to the circumstances in which they live—that one of the worst parts about deep deprivation is that it robs people of the aspirations and dissatisfactions connected with a robust sense of their own dignity.[56] The "Hands" in the Coketown factory do manifest some discontent; but given their exhaustion, the material and imaginative limitations under which they labor, they seem likely to welcome any small relief, and to accept a very inadequate and insensitive leadership, since they have not been able to form the ideal of full equality. Stephen can see that his life is "a muddle," but he cannot clearly articulate the nature of his discontent or fully feel its force. Gradgrind, on the other hand, is very satisfied with his life, which the novel shows to be spiritually impoverished, and his discontent at the novel's end is clearly progress over his early equanimity.

At the limit, the character Bitzer shows us the extreme unreliability of the feeling of satisfaction when not linked to any more probing ethical evaluation, for whatever makes that empty vessel of self-interest feel pleased fills the reader with anxiety and even horror. We know right from the start that there is more worth, more humanity, in Sissy Jupe's misery and discomfort—a sensitive barometer of cant and injustice—than in Bitzer's empty complacency. "Whereas the girl was so dark-eyed and dark-haired, that she seemed to receive a deeper and more lustrous color from the sun when it shone upon her, the boy was so light-eyed and light-haired that the self-same rays appeared to draw out of him what little color he ever possessed." In this eloquent description, the novel expresses the human richness of Sissy's response to life, including her unhappiness, and the ghastly mechanical quality of Bitzer's optimism.[57] Can utility give us the measure of these lives, of the education of which they are the fruit, and the human functioning they do and do not contain?

Such criticisms of utility as a measure—together with the other points I have mentioned about aggregation and qualitative differences, which have been much stressed in recent philosophical critiques of economics—have led a group of economists and philosophers in the development sphere to defend an approach to quality of life measurement based on a notion of human functioning and human capability, rather than on either opulence or utility. (This approach was pioneered within economics by Amartya Sen, who is also a philosopher.)[58] The idea is to ask how well people are doing by asking how well their form of life has enabled them to function in a variety of distinct areas, including, but not limited to, mobility, health, education, political participation, and social relations. This approach refuses to come up with a single number, reducing quality to quantity. And it insists on asking about the actual functional capabilities of each distinct and qualitatively different individual, rather than simply about how much in terms of resources an individual commands. This is so because the approach recognizes that individuals need varying amounts of resources in order to arrive at the same level of functioning: the handicapped person more resources to be mobile than the person of ordinary mobility, the large and active person more food than the small and sedentary person, and so forth.[59] Nonetheless, the approach does encourage modeling and measurement: as when one studies the access that mobility-impaired people do and do not have to functions of various sorts in a given society; as when one studies the different food needs of people of different sizes, ages, and occupations; as when one studies the ways in which class distinctions impede access to political participation. The governments of Finland and Sweden actually use such plural quality-based measures to study inequalities in their populations—proving, by doing so, that it is possible to measure effectively in this way.[60] Such measures will indeed be plural and not single, qualitatively diverse rather than homogeneous. This, Sen and I argue (within limits) makes them better, not worse.

What I now wish to claim is that a novel like *Hard Times* is a paradigm of such assessment. Presenting the life of a population with a rich variety of qualitative distinctions and complex individual descriptions of functioning and impediments to functioning, using a general notion of human need and human functioning in a highly concrete context, it provides the sort of information required to assess quality of life and involves its reader in the task of making the assessment. Thus it displays the kind of imaginative framework for public work in this sphere within which any more quantitative and simplified model should be formulated. At the same time, it both exemplifies and cultivates abilities of imagination that are essential to the intelligent making of such assessments, in public as well as private life.

Hard Times ends by invoking one of its most central characters: "Dear reader! It rests with you and me, whether, in our two fields of action, similar things shall be or not. Let them be! We shall sit with lighter bosoms on the hearth, to see the ashes of our fires turn gray and cold." Addressing the reader as a friend and fellow agent, though in a different sphere of life, the authorial voice turns readers' sympathetic wonder at the fates of the characters back on themselves, reminding them that they too are on the way to death, that they too have but this one chance to see in the fire the shapes of fancy and thee prospects they suggest for the improvement of human life. The novel is right: it does rest with us whether such things shall be or not. Its claim is that the literary imagination is an essential part of both the theory and the practice of citizenship.

3

Rational Emotions

"Bitzer," said Mr. Gradgrind, broken down, and miserably submissive to him, *"have you a heart?"*

"The circulation, sir," returned Bitzer, smiling at the oddity of the question, *"couldn't be carried on without one. No man, sir, acquainted with the facts established by Harvey relating to the circulation of the blood, can doubt that I have a heart."*

"Is it accessible," cried Mr. Gradgrind, *"to any compassionate influence?"*

"It is accessible to Reason, sir," returned the excellent young man. *"And to nothing else."*

Charles Dickens, *Hard Times*

Reason and Nothing Else

Literature is in league with the emotions. Readers of novels, spectators of dramas, find themselves led by these works to fear, to grief, to pity, to anger, to joy and delight, even to passionate love. Emotions are not just likely responses to the content of many literary works; they are built into their very structure, as ways in which literary forms solicit attention. Plato, describing the "ancient quarrel" between the poets and the philosophers, saw this clearly: epic and tragic poets lure their audience by presenting heroes who are not self-sufficient, and who therefore suffer deeply when calamity befalls. Forming bonds of both sympathy and identification, they cause the reader or spectator to experience pity and fear for the hero's plight, fear, too, for themselves, insofar as their own possibilities are seen as similar to those of the hero. Plato saw correctly that it was no trivial matter to remove those (to him) objectionable

53

emotional elements from tragedy, for they inform the genre itself, its sense of what has importance, what a suitable plot is, what needs recognition as a salient part of human life. To take the emotive elements away, you must rewrite the plot, reshape the characters, and restructure the nature of the interest that holds the spectator to the unfolding story (or, if sufficiently altered, non-story).

One can make a similar point about the realist novel. As Dickens says, such novels are stories of "human hopes and fears." The interest and pleasure they offer is inseparable from the readers' compassionate concern for "men and women like themselves" and the conflicts and reversals that beset them. But then a lover of literature who wishes to question Plato's banishment of literary artists from the public realm must, in pleading her case, make some defense of the emotions and their contribution to public rationality.

Today, too, they badly need defending. The contrast Bitzer draws between emotion and reason has become a commonplace of our public discourse, although its conceptual value is marred both by a failure to define what emotions are and by equivocation between a descriptive and a normative use of "reason" and "rational." Bitzer takes for granted that reason is defined in terms of the Gradgrind economic conception, according to which reason does indeed exclude emotive elements such as sympathy and gratitude. Then this highly controversial conception is used without further defense as if it were a norm, so that whatever it excludes can be from then on treated as dispensable or even contemptible. "It is accessible to Reason, sir, and to nothing else," he proudly boasts of his heart.

Bitzer's contemporary heirs are quick to make the same move. Thus in his 1981 book *The Economics of Justice*, Richard Posner, leading thinker of the law-and-economics movement, begins by announcing that he will assume "that people are rational maximizers of satisfactions." Without defending this conception of the rational, he then justifies his proposed extension of economic analysis to all areas of human life by appealing to the conception as if it were an established norm, and as if this norm excludes all emotion-based decision-making:

> Is it plausible to suppose that people are rational only or mainly when they are transacting in markets, and not when they are engaged in other activities of life, such as marriage and litigation and crime and discrimination and concealment of personal information? . . . But many readers will, I am

sure, intuitively regard these choices . . . as lying within the area where decisions are emotional rather than rational.[1]

In other words, we can respect people's choices as rational in the normative sense only if we can show that they conform to the utilitarian rational-
maximizing conception and do not reflect the influence of emotional
factors. (Posner offers us no account of the emotions or of their relationship
to belief.) According to this conception, works like Dickens's novel, which
suggests that emotions of certain sorts are frequently essential elements in a
good decision, would be misleading and pernicious works—"bad books"
indeed, as Mr. Gradgrind zealously stated.

Nor is this denigration of emotion confined to theoretical utilitarian
works on public rationality. In one or another form, it plays an important
part in public practice. Consider, for example, a jury instruction issued by
the state of California. At the penalty phase, the jury is cautioned that it
"must not be swayed by mere sentiment, conjecture, sympathy, passion,
prejudice, public opinion or public feeling."[2] As Justice Brennan demonstrated with a wealth of examples, such instructions are generally understood by both prosecutors and jurors to entail that the juror completely disregard emotional factors in reaching a decision. In a representative case, the
jury was informed that its assessment of aggravating and mitigating factors
"is not a question, I believe, that should be guided by emotion, sympathy,
pity, anger, hate, or anything like that because it is not rational if you make
a decision on that kind of basis." The prosecutor continues: "It would be
very hard to completely filter out all our emotions, make the decision on a
rational basis"—but that, he adds, is what a good juror will do.[3] This filtering process would exclude, as Brennan persuasively argues, factors of sympathetic assessment of the defendant's background and character that are
actually indispensable to a rational judgment about sentencing, and a central part of what such judgments have traditionally been understood to involve. Getting clear about the unexamined contrast between emotion and
reason thus makes a practical difference in the law.[4]

Objecting to Emotions

In order to answer the charge that emotions are in a normative sense irrational and thus inappropriate as guides in public deliberation, I must, first of

all, make the charge more precise. A number of very different arguments have been made against the emotions, all of which can be expressed using the convenient umbrella term "irrational." In some cases, these arguments are not only distinct, but also built on incompatible views of what emotions are. So any defense must begin by disentangling them. I shall focus on only four of the much larger family of objections that can be found. But these are, I believe, the most germane to the debate about the public role of literature.

First, then, there is the objection that the emotions are blind forces that have nothing (or nothing much) to do with reasoning. Like gusts of wind or the swelling currents of the sea, they push the agent around, surd unthinking energies. They do not themselves embody reflection or judgment, and they are not very responsive to the judgments of reason. (This picture of emotion is sometimes expressed by describing emotions as "animal," as elements of a not fully human nature in us. It has also been linked with the idea that emotions are somehow "female" and reason "male"—presumably because the female is taken to be closer to the animal and instinctual, more immersed in the body.) It is easy to see how this view of emotions would lead to their dismissal from the life of the deliberating citizen and the good judge. Forces of the sort described do seem to be a threat to good judgment, and their dominance in an individual would indeed seem to call into question the fitness of that individual for the functions of citizenship.

A very different argument is made in the chief antiemotion works of the Western philosophical tradition. Variants of it can be found in Plato, Epicurus, the Greek and Roman Stoics, and Spinoza. These philosophers all hold a view of emotions incompatible with the view that underlies the first objection. They hold, namely, that emotions are very closely related to (or in some cases identical with) judgments. So lack of judgment is not at all their problem. The problem, however, is that the judgments are false. They are false because they ascribe a very high value to external persons and events that are not fully controlled by the person's virtue or rational will. They are acknowledgments, then, of the person's own incompleteness and vulnerability. Fear involves the thought that there are important bad things that could happen in the future and that one is not fully capable of preventing them. Grief involves the thought that someone or something extremely important has been taken from one; anger the thought that another has seriously damaged something to which one attaches great worth; pity the thought that others are suffering in a nontrivial way, through no fault of their own or beyond their fault; hope involves the thought that one's future good is not fully under one's control.

In all of these cases, the emotions picture human life as something needy and incomplete, something that has hostages to fortune. Ties to children, parents, loved ones, fellow citizens, country, one's own body and health— these are the material on which emotions work; and these ties, given the power of chance to disrupt them, make human life a vulnerable business, in which complete control is neither possible nor, given the value of these attachments for the person who has them, even desirable. But according to the antiemotion philosophers, that picture of the world is in fact false. As Socrates said, "The good person cannot be harmed." Virtue and thought are the only things of real worth, and one's virtue and thought cannot be damaged by fortune. Another way of expressing this is to say that the good person is completely self-sufficient.

This argument is sometimes connected with a relative of the first argument, through the idea of stability.[5] A good judge, these philosophers insist, is someone stable, someone who cannot be swayed by the currents of fortune or fashion. But people in the grip of emotions, because they place important elements of their good outside themselves, will change with the gusts of fortune and are just as little to be relied upon as the world itself is. Now hopeful, now in tears, now serene, now plunged into violent grief, they lack the stability and solidity of the wise person, who takes a constant and calm delight in the unswerving course of his own virtue. Thus this second picture can lead to some of the same conclusions as the first. But it is important to notice how different, in the two cases, the reasons for the conclusions are. On the first view, emotions are neither taught nor embodied in beliefs; on the second, they are taught along with evaluative beliefs. On the first, they can be neither educated nor entirely removed; on the second, both are possible. On the first, emotions are unstable because of their unthinking internal structure; on the second, because they are thoughts that attach importance to unstable external things.

This second objection is what led Plato to urge that most existing literature be banned from the ideal city; it led the Stoics to urge their pupils to pay attention to literature only from a viewpoint of secure critical detachment—like Odysseus, they said, lashed to the mast so that he could hear, but not be swayed by, the sirens' song. It led Spinoza to select a form of communication with his reader as far from the literary as possible: the geometrical method, in which, as he says, "I shall regard human actions and desires exactly as if I were dealing with lines, planes, and bodies." As all of these writers saw, most great literature treats the events that befall finite and vulnerable people as deeply significant, involving the audience in their good or ill fortune. It shows a hero like Achilles grieving for the death of Patroclus, rolling in the dirt and crying out, rather than recognizing that such things have no true importance. Thus it elicits bad desires in the very act of reading or watching, and it gives the audience bad paradigms to take into their lives. Once again, we should insist that this is not a point about literary *content* simply, but a point about *form:* for the tragic genre, as we have said, is committed to grief, pity, and fear. Thus its very shape, its characteristic choices of character and plot-structure, are subversive of philosophical attempts to teach rational self-sufficiency.

As will become clear in what follows, I very much prefer the second objector's view to the first, in the sense that I think it is based on a far more profound and better-argued view of the relationship between emotion and belief or judgment. But it should already be plain that one might accept this analysis of the emotions and yet refuse to accept the Stoic conclusion that the emotions are (in the normative sense) irrational and totally to be avoided when we seek to deliberate rationally. For, as one can see, that conclusion is based on a substantive and highly controversial ethical view, according to which ties to loved ones, country, and other undependable items outside the self are without true worth. But one might dispute this. And then one would wish to retain any evaluative judgments contained in emotions that one has judged to be true, and to draw on those judgments in practical reasoning.[6]

A third objection, while compatible with some respect for the emotions in private life, assails their role in public deliberation. (It is compatible with the second objector's analysis of emotions as closely linked to judgments about the worth of external objects, and probably not compatible with the first objector's claim that they are altogether without thought.) Emotions, this objector charges, focus on the person's actual ties or attachments, especially to concrete objects or people close to the self. They consider the object not abstractly, as one among many, but as special—and special, in part at least, on account of its prominence in the agent's own life. Emotions always stay close to home and contain, so to speak, a first-person reference. Thus love ascribes great worth to a person who is in an intimate relationship with the agent, and its intensity usually depends on the existence of a connection of some sort between agent and object. Grief, again, is grief for a loss that is felt as cutting at the roots of one's life. Fear is usually either completely self-centered or felt on behalf of friends, family, loved ones. Anger is aroused by slights or damages to something that is important to oneself. In all these cases, emotions bind the moral imagination to particulars that lie close to the self. They do not look at human worth or even human suffering in an even-handed way. They do not get worked up about distant lives, unseen sufferings. This, from the point of view of both utilitarian and Kantian moral theory, would be a good reason to reject them from a public norm of rationality, even though they might still have some value in the home. Even pity, which initially looks more universal, may not be so: for on Aristotle's analysis at least, it too contains a first-person reference, in the thought that one's own possibilities are similar to those of the sufferer. On this view, then, novels, by arousing and strengthening emotions, would be encouraging a self-centered and unequal form of attention to the sufferings of other human beings. We should prefer the impartiality of the calculative intellect, and of the prose in which it is embodied: for here each person counts for one, and none for more than one.

Closely related, the fourth objection is that emotions are too much concerned with particulars and not sufficiently with larger social units, such as classes. This is a point that has seemed to many Marxists, and to other political thinkers as well, to make the novel an altogether unsuitable instrument for political reflection—or in some versions, an instrument so committed to bourgeois individualism that it is unsuited for critical political reflection. Irving Howe made this point against Henry James, alleging that his insistence on a fine-tuned perception of particulars, his close scrutiny of subtle emotions, betrayed an incapacity for understanding the political, which is "a collective mode of action."[7] In Doris Lessing's *The Golden Notebook*, the heroine, a Marxist novelist, faces a related objection from her Marxist friends: that her attachment to the novel and its emotional structures betrays a residual attachment to the bourgeois world and is inconsistent with her politics. On some versions of this objection, novels may be useful enough in the private domain, so long as they do not overstep their bounds; on the

Marxist version, which does not grant the existence of an ethical domain separate from the political, they are altogether worthless.

Each of these four objections is a profound one. To answer them all definitively would require me to elaborate and defend a full theory of the emotions. This obviously cannot be done here.[8] Instead, I shall map out plausible answers to the four objections and then ask how public emotions might best be filtered or winnowed in order to make sure that we are relying on the truly trustworthy ones.

Answering the Objections

Emotions as Blind Animal Forces

The first objector insists that emotions are irrational in the normative sense, that is, bad guides to choice, because they do not partake of reason in even the broadest descriptive sense. Emotions are just blind impulses that neither contain a perception of their object nor rest upon beliefs. This position is in one sense, I feel, hardly worth spending time on, since it has never been strongly supported by major philosophers who have done a great deal of their most serious work on the emotions—including those who for other reasons dislike the emotions intensely. By now it has been widely discredited even where it once was popular, in cognitive psychology, for example, and in anthropology.[9] But it still has a hold on much informal thinking and talking about emotions, which retains the legacy of earlier behaviorist and empiricist theories. Therefore it seems important to say something about what has led to the widespread conclusion that it is not a tenable view.

Western philosophers as diverse as Plato, Aristotle, the Greek and Roman Stoics, Spinoza, and Adam Smith have agreed that it is very important to distinguish emotions such as grief, love, fear, pity, anger, and hope from bodily impulses and drives such as hunger and thirst.[10] This distinction is made in two ways. First, emotions contain within themselves a directedness toward an object, and within the emotion the object is viewed under an intentional description. That is to say, it figures in the emotion as it appears to, is perceived by, the person who experiences the emotion. My anger is not simply an impulse, a boiling of the blood: it is directed at someone, namely, a person who is seen as having wronged me. The way I see the person is itself intrinsic to the nature of my emotion. Gratitude contains an opposed view of another person's relation to my good; distinguishing anger from gratitude requires giving an account of these opposed perceptions. Love is not, in the relevant sense, blind: it perceives its object as endowed with a special wonder and importance. Once again, this way of perceiving the object is essential to the character of the emotion. Hatred differs from love in nothing so much as the opposed character of its perceptions. Emotions, in short, whatever else they are, are at least in part ways of perceiving.

Second, emotions are also intimately connected with certain beliefs about their object. The philosophical tradition I have mentioned is not unanimous about the precise relation between emotion and belief. Some hold that the relevant beliefs are necessary conditions for the emotion, some that they are both necessary and sufficient, some that they are constituent parts of what the emotion is, some that the emotion is just a certain sort of belief or judgment. Let us begin, therefore, with the weakest view, on which all agree: the view that emotions are so responsive to beliefs of certain sorts that they cannot come into being without them. What leads these philosophers to accept that view? Consider, again, the emotion of anger. Being angry seems to require the belief that I, or something or someone important to me, have been wronged or harmed by another person's intentional action. If any significant aspect of that complex belief should cease to seem true to me—if I change my view about who has done the harm, or about whether it was intentional, or about whether what happened was in fact a harm, my anger can be expected to abate or to change its course accordingly. Much the same is true of other major emotions. Fear requires the belief that important damages may happen to me or someone important to me in the future, and that I am not fully in control of warding them off. Pity requires the belief that another person is suffering in some significant way, through no fault of her own or beyond her fault, and so forth. Some of the beliefs in question, especially those concerned with value or importance, may be very deeply rooted in one's psychology; getting rid of them cannot be expected to be the job of a one-shot argument. But without these beliefs, no emotion can take root.

Most of the thinkers in the tradition go further, holding that the beliefs in question are also constituent parts of the emotion, part of what identifies it and sets it apart from other emotions. It seems highly implausible that we can individuate and define complex emotions such as anger, fear, and pity simply by reference to the way they feel. To tell whether a certain pain is fear or grief, we have to inspect the beliefs that are bound up in the experience. To tell whether a certain happy feeling should be called love or gratitude—again, we must inspect not just the feeling, but also the beliefs that go with it. For this reason, definitions of emotion in the philosophical tradition standardly include beliefs as well as feelings.

It appears to many thinkers, furthermore, that the beliefs we have mentioned are—usually, at any rate—sufficient for the emotion. That is, if I really succeed in making you believe that B has been insulting you behind your back, and you believe that insults of that type are important damages, that will suffice to make you angry with B. I do not need, as well, to light a fire under your heart. Whatever fire there is, is fire about the insult and is sufficiently produced by awareness of the insult. Much of the ancient science of rhetoric rests on this observation, and modern political speech is no stranger to it either. When George Bush wanted to make the American public fear the prospect of a Dukakis presidency, he did not need to inject ice water into their veins. All he needed to do was to make them believe that a Dukakis presidency would mean significant dangers for them that they would be powerless to ward off—namely, Willie Hortons running free in the streets of every city, ready to prey on innocent women and children. This position is compatible with the view that emotions have other noncognitive components (such as feelings or bodily states) in addition to beliefs, but it insists that the relevant beliefs are sufficient causes of these further components.

The greatest Stoic thinker, Chrysippus, went one step further, holding that emotions are simply identical with a certain type of belief or judgment. No specific feeling or bodily state is absolutely necessary for a given type of emotion. His position is, I believe, a powerful one, and far less counterintuitive than we might at first think.[11] But since it is an intricate matter to defend it, and since the weaker cognitive views of emotion are all we need to rebut the first objector, I shall forgo that task here.

Notice that the family of cognitive views I have laid out still makes ample room for saying of some (or even perhaps of all) emotions that they are, in the normative sense, irrational, for emotions must now be assessed by inspecting the relevant beliefs or judgments. These may be either true or false, either appropriate or inappropriate to their object, and they may be either rational or irrational. (These are two independent dimensions of assessment:

a belief might be false but rational, if I formed it on the basis of good evidence, but it happens to be wrong; it may also, and more often, be true but irrational, if I formed it hastily and uncritically, but it happens to be the case.) But in no case will emotions be irrational in the sense of being totally cut off from cognition and judgment.

It is important to notice that it is this way of assessing emotions—one that grants their cognitive content and then asks how appropriate they are to their object and situation—that has been the dominant tradition in the criminal law, where the common-law formulation of the notion of reasonable provocation, to take just one example, appraises the appropriateness of a defendant's anger to the situation, by asking what the response of a reasonable person in that situation would be. Some events are judged to be events that would provoke a reasonable person to extreme anger—for example, an attack on one's child. This anger and its consequences will be differently treated by the law from the anger of someone who is just an ill-tempered and uncontrolled character. Even though the "reasonably provoked" person who commits an act of violence as a result will still be convicted of a crime (unless the violent act is shown to have been in self-defense), the existence of reasonable provocation will be likely to reduce the level of the offense— from murder, for example, to voluntary manslaughter. In these and other ways, the common-law tradition treats emotions not as blind forces that can overwhelm volition by sheer strength, but as elements of a person's character; it is assumed that people are responsible for modifying their emotions to make them parts of a reasonable person's character.[12]

In short, there is no more reason to think emotions unsuited for deliberation just because they can go wrong, than there is reason to dismiss all beliefs from deliberation just because they can go wrong. There might of course be an argument that this class of cognitive attitudes is for some reason especially likely to go wrong—whether because of its content or the manner of its formation. But such an argument would have to be produced and assessed. To the assessment of the most famous such argument I now turn.

Emotions as Acknowledgments of Neediness

I now turn to the second objector, the ancient Stoic. In answering the first objector, I have endorsed the Stoic account of what emotions are, finding in them both object-directed intentionality and a close relation to beliefs of a certain sort, beliefs that ascribe high importance to things and persons outside the self's secure control. To make these judgments of worth is to acknowledge one's own neediness and lack of self-sufficiency. We can now locate the cognitive dimension of the emotions more precisely: they enable the agent to perceive a certain sort of worth or value. For those to whom such things really do have worth, emotions will be necessary for a complete ethical vision. Louisa Gradgrind says that, lacking emotion, she has been "stone blind." Her blindness has been a value-blindness, an inability to see the worth and importance of things outside herself, to see what she needs and what she doesn't, to see where her life needs to be completed by ties to others.

But are such acknowledgments of neediness and incompleteness good? The Stoic objector states that beliefs that people have deep needs from the world are always false: the only resources one really needs come from within oneself and one's own virtue. These false beliefs are, moreover, socially damaging, sapping confidence and robbing action of its stability. One can get rid of them, and life will be more satisfactory as a result. This means, for the Stoics, radically rewriting the vision of the world that their young pupils would have absorbed from their literary education. Instead of dramatic stories, they say, we should have paradigms of self-sufficiency and detachment, since a good person's life contains no dramatic suspense or tension. "Behold how tragedy comes about," writes the Stoic Epictetus, "When chance events befall fools." Socrates' calm demeanor in prison shows the way a wise person will greet misfortune. This example becomes Stoicism's antitragic ideal of the hero. About Socrates no conventional literary work can be written, for Socrates does not treat the events around him as worthy of much regard. The only "plot" in which he takes an interest is the unfolding of the argument, but this, Stoics hold, is always within his power.

This is a profound vision of the ethical life—profound, first of all, because it is based on a powerful conception of what emotions are, one that I believe to be more or less correct; profound, as well, because it raises deep questions about what a good human life should be, what sorts of vulnerabilities are compatible with the constancy that the ethical and political life require. And the view is profound, finally, because, like all the most searching philosophical thought, it shows its own argumentative structure to the reader and thus shows, as well, how and where one might take issue with it. In particular, it shows both friends and opponents of the emotions that the radical antiemotion conclusion rests on normative claims about self-sufficiency and detachment that are highly controversial. Let me at least begin to question those premises.

Consider the emotion of compassion (pity).[13] As Aristotle long ago argued, this emotion requires the belief that another person is suffering in a serious way through no fault of her own, or beyond her fault. Those who feel compassion must also, in most cases at least, believe that their own possibilities (or as Aristotle adds, those of someone they love) are, broadly speaking, similar to those of the sufferer. This acknowledgment that one might oneself suffer similar things is traditionally and plausibly linked with beneficence, and the refusal of pity (as in Dickens's Bitzer) with a hard and ungenerous disposition.

The foundation of compassion (as of its near relative, fear) is the belief that many common forms of bad luck—losses of children and other loved ones, the hardships of war, the loss of political rights, bodily illness and deficiency, the prospect of one's own death—are in fact of major importance. In order to remove compassion and its relatives from human life, the Stoics must remove that fundamental belief. But then we must ask what reasons they give us to care profoundly about the bad things that happen to others, what reasons to get involved, to take risks, for the sake of social justice and beneficence.

It has always been difficult for philosophies based on an idea of the self-sufficiency of virtue to explain why beneficence matters. No major thinker of this sort is willing to say that it does not matter; and yet for Socrates, for the Greek and Roman Stoics, for Spinoza, for Kant, it is difficult to motivate it consistently, given the alleged moral irrelevance of external goods, the self-sufficiency of virtuous will. Repudiating pity, as the Stoics do, leaves few motives for the acts usually prompted by pity; and if they are performed out of very different motives, say on account of pious obedience to Zeus's will, it is not clear that their moral character is the same. In effect, the person deprived of the evaluations contained in pity seems to be deprived of ethical information without which such situations cannot be adequately, rationally appraised.

The moral vision of Dickens's novel, by contrast—as of most mainstream realist novels and tragic dramas—begins from the profound importance of the vulnerabilities of human life and its need for "external goods." It begins, therefore, from fear, gratitude, and pity or compassion. Indeed, we can say of the mainstream realist novel what Aristotle said of tragic drama: that the very form constructs compassion in readers, positioning them as people who care intensely about the sufferings and bad luck of others, and who identify with them in ways that show possibilities for themselves. Like tragic spectators, novel-readers have both empathy with the plight of the characters, experiencing what happens to them as if from their point of view, and also pity, which goes beyond empathy in that it involves a spectatorial judgment that the characters' misfortunes are indeed serious and have indeed arisen not through their fault. Such judgments are not always available within the empathetic viewpoint, so the novel-reader, like a tragic spectator, must alternate between identification and a more external sort of sympathy. What the ancient pity tradition claims for epic and tragedy might now be claimed for the novel: that this complex cast of mind is essential in order to take the full measure of the adversity and suffering of others, and that this appraisal is necessary for full social rationality. Rousseau shrewdly observes that the absence of a belief in one's own potential vulnerability can easily lead to social obtuseness and unresponsiveness:

> Why are kings without pity for their subjects? It is because they count on never being human beings. Why are the rich so harsh to the poor? It is because they do not have fear of becoming poor. Why does a noble have such contempt for a peasant? It is because he never will *be* a peasant. . . . It is the weakness of the human being that makes it sociable, it is our common sufferings that carry our hearts to humanity; we would owe it nothing if we were not humans. Every attachment is a sign of insufficiency. . . . Thus from our weakness itself, our fragile happiness is born. (*Émile*, bk. 4)

Utilitarianism takes its start from the fact of common suffering and is, at its best, motivated by a wish to relieve pain. So it is a very serious internal criticism of utilitarianism if it can be shown that the ways of reasoning it designates as "rational," by excluding emotion, deprive us of information we need if we are to have a fully rational response to the suffering of others.

Hard Times pursues these criticisms, showing that it is only when Mr. Gradgrind becomes aware of his own need and feels "a wretched sense of helplessness" that he is able to address productively the needs of those around him. By contrast, Bitzer, for whom all human relationships are market transactions and gratitude an irrational, "untenable" response, fails to be a good Utilitarian agent in the sense of the original motivations of that view, since he fails utterly to comprehend and respond to another person's pain.[14]

In short, if we reject the Stoic tradition in the matter of self-sufficiency, we must, to be consistent, reject its normative arguments for the dismissal of emotion. There might be other arguments for the dismissal, but these will need to come forward for adjudication. Meanwhile, it would appear that many emotional responses embody correct perceptions of value, worthy of guiding deliberation: for example, the correct evaluation of the importance of children and other loved ones in a person's life. And one can go further. If one agrees with most of the philosophical tradition in holding that certain sorts of beliefs about the importance of worldly events and persons are not only necessary, but also sufficient, for emotion—and this seems to be a very plausible position[15]—then one will have to grant that if emotion is not there, those beliefs are not (or not fully) there. And that means that a part of social rationality is not fully there. Those who accept the judgments about the value of the "goods of fortune" that the Aristotle/Rousseau tradition puts forward against the Stoics must, if consistent, admit emotions as essential elements in good reasoning about these matters. Thus judges or jurors, who deny themselves the influence of emotion deny themselves ways of seeing the world that seem essential to seeing it completely. It cannot be (normatively) rational to think this way—even when we are doing economics!

Emotions and Impartiality

The calculating intellect claims to be impartial and capable of strict numerical justice, while emotions, it alleges, are prejudiced, unduly partial to the close at hand. Each human being should count as one, and none as more than one, the utilitarian plausibly insists. But in the emotions attachments to family and close friends seem all-encompassing, blotting out the fair claims of the distant many. So, too, the reader of novels, taught to cherish particular characters rather than to think of the whole world, receives a moral formation subversive of justice.

This we may doubt. As I argued in chapter 2, the abstract vision of the calculating intellect proves relatively short-sighted and undiscriminating, unless aided by the vivid and empathetic imagining of what it is really like to live a certain sort of life. I can now add that emotions are an integral part of this more comprehensive vision. Louisa complains that her father's failure to educate the emotions has made her "unjust," and we see, in truth, that the absence of a quick intelligence of others' misery has in fact made her very slow to grasp the situation of the Coketown workers. By contrast, Sissy's robust emotional responses to the needs of others are essential ingredients in her ability (in her economics lesson) to come up with sensible answers about distant hypothetical cases. Let us now consider two further examples from that lesson.

Sissy is told by her utilitarian teacher that in "an immense town" of a million inhabitants only twenty-five are starved to death in the streets. The teacher, M'Choakumchild, asks her what she thinks about this—plainly expecting an answer expressing satisfaction that the numbers are so low. Sissy's response, however, is that "it must be just as hard upon those who were starved, whether the others were a million, or a million million." Again, told that in a given period of time a hundred thousand people took sea voyages and only five hundred drowned, Sissy remarks that this low percentage is "nothing to the relations and friends of the people who were killed." In both of these cases, the numerical analysis comforts and distances: what a fine low percentage, says M'Choakumchild, and no action, clearly, need be taken about that. Intellect without emotions is, we might say, value-blind: it lacks the sense of the meaning and worth of a person's death that the judgments internal to emotions would have supplied. Sissy's emotional response invests the dead with the worth of humanity. Feeling what starvation is for the starving, loss for the grief-stricken, she says, quite rightly, that the low numbers don't buy off those deaths, that complacency simply on account of the low number is not the right response. Because she is always aware that there is no replacing a dead human being, she thinks that the people in charge of sea voyages had better try harder. Dealing with numbers it is easy to say, "This figure is all right"—for none of these numbers has any nonarbitrary meaning. (And really, notice that 500 deaths out of 100,000 is incredibly high for ocean crossings, whether by sea or air.) Dealing with imagined and felt human lives, one will (other things equal) accept no figures of starvation as simply all right, no statistics of passenger safety as simply acceptable (though of course one might judge that other factors make further progress on these matters for the present unwise or impossible). The emotions do not tell us how to solve these problems; they do keep our attention focused on them as problems we ought to solve. Judge which approach would lead to a better public response to a famine at a distance, to the situation of the homeless, to product testing and safety standards.

This does not mean that one would not use economic models of the familiar type. Frequently in such cases they can provide valuable information. But one's use of them would be steered by a sense of human value. Nor need emotion-based reasoning hold that human life is "sacred" or "of infinite value," vague notions that probably do not capture many people's intuitions when these are closely examined, and that have generated much confusion in arguments about animal rights, the termination of life, the treatment of severely handicapped humans.[16] We may concede that in some of these cases the emotion-based vision of a single death might distort judgment if steered by such a vague notion of infinite value, and that the "cold" techniques of economics might give more accurate guidance. (For example, we certainly should be ready to accept a relatively low risk of death or disease to attain considerable social gains.) But in this case, I claim, what we are saying is not that the calculation per se is more reliable than emotion per se: we are saying instead that a certain degree of detachment from the immediate—which calculation may help to foster in some people—can sometimes enable us to sort out our beliefs and intuitions better and thus to get a more refined sense of what our emotions actually are, and which among them are the most reliable. If we had only numbers to play with, and lacked the sense of value embodied in emotions of fear and compassion, we would not have any nonarbitrary way of answering such questions. (To the issue of detachment I shall shortly return.)

We may add to this general argument a genetic thesis. Intimate bonds of love and gratitude between a child and its parents, formed in infancy and nourished in childhood, seem to be indispensable starting points for an adult's ability to do good in the wider social world. These initial attachments need further education, to be sure, but they must be there if anything good is to come of education. This point is at least as old, in the Western tradition, as Aristotle's criticism of Plato in book 2 of the *Politics*. Aristotle insists that removing the family, rather than ensuring impartial and equal concern for all citizens, will ensure that nobody cares strongly about anything. The point is vividly developed in *Hard Times*, in Dickens's chilling account of the education of the young Gradgrind children, who are taught to calculate but never encouraged to love. And the story of Louisa's tragic collapse shows us something further: that a reliance on emotion in the developmental process can actually (by providing good guidance about important attachments) diminish the more damaging kinds of need and vulnerability in later life, creating a personality that has a more stable center than a personality raised in Louisa's way, a personality that has balanced emotional commitments and therefore balanced practical judgments. Repression of childhood emotion, by contrast, may simply bring emotion back in a more destructive and genuinely irrational form.[17]

Emotions and Classes

As for the related objection, that the emotions are too concerned with the individual, too little with larger social units such as classes, we must grant that in fact the whole commitment of the novel as genre, and not least of its emotional elements, is indeed to the individual, seen as both qualitatively distinct and separate. In this sense, the vision of community embodied in the novel is, as Lionel Trilling long ago argued, a liberal vision, in which individuals are seen as valuable in their own right, and as having distinctive stories of their own to tell.[18] While the genre emphasizes the mutual interdependence of persons, showing the world as one in which we are all implicated in one another's good and ill, it also insists on respecting the separate life of each person, and on seeing the person as a separate center of experience.

It is in that sense no accident that mass movements frequently fare badly in the novel, to the extent that they neglect the separate agency of their members, their privacy, and their qualitative differences. The British bureaucracy in *Little Dorrit*, the trade union movement in *Hard Times*, the divorce laws that cause Stephen Blackpool's misery, the entire legal system in *Bleak House*, the revolutionary movement in Henry James's *The Princess Casamassima*—all are seen as guilty of obtuseness toward the individual. To the extent that they are guilty, the novel in its very form is bound to be their enemy and subverter. This means that from the point of view of such movements the novel is a dangerously reactionary form—as the Communist friends of Doris Lessing's novelist heroine in *The Golden Notebook* are eager to observe, as Lukács was quick to emphasize when he condemned as "petit bourgeois" the liberal-cosmopolitan political vision of Rabindranath Tagore's novel *The Home and the World*.[19]

This political attitude has its dangers, and sometimes the novelist's suspiciousness of any form of collective action leads to error—as when, in *Hard Times*, Dickens seems to suggest that it would be better to divert and entertain the workers rather than to change, through trade union action, the conditions of their labor; as when he portrays trade unions as in their very nature repressive toward individual workers. But such a failure in no way indicts the whole approach. More often, I think, the vision of individual life quality afforded by novels proves compatible with, and actually motivates, serious institutional and political criticism—as when, in Sissy Jupe's lesson, the reader's emotions themselves indicate the meaning of the hunger and misery of millions, directing the calculative intellect to interpret the numbers in an urgently activist spirit; as when, in Tagore's mordant portrayal of Indian nationalism, we find the movement's leaders neglecting, in their abstract zeal, the real economic misery of the poor traders who cannot earn a living unless they sell the cheaper foreign wares, while we, with the author's surrogate Nikhil, understand better what it really is to make each human life count for one.[20]

It seems appropriate, in fact, for any form of collective action to bear in mind, as an ideal, the full accountability to the needs and particular circumstances of the individual that the novel recommends, in its form as well as its content. This does not entail a romanticism that scorns modeling and measurement, as I have insisted repeatedly. Such "literary" insights underlie much of what is best in recent economic approaches to the measurement of the quality of life. A story of human life quality, without stories of individual human actors, would, I argued, be too indeterminate to show how resources actually work in promoting various types of human functioning. Similarly, a story of class action, without the stories of individuals, would not show us the point and meaning of class actions, which is always the amelioration of individual lives. Raymond Williams puts this point very well, defending traditional realist narrative against socialist criticism:

Moreover we should not, as socialists, make the extraordinary error of be-
lieving that most people only become interesting when they begin to engage
with political and industrial actions of a previously recognized kind. That
error deserved Sartre's jibe that for many Marxists people are born only
when they first enter capitalist employment. For if we are serious about even
political life we have to enter that world in which people live as they can as
themselves, and then necessarily live within a whole complex of work and
love and illness and natural beauty. If we are serious socialists, we shall then
often find within and cutting across this real substance—always, in its details, so surprising and often vivid—the profound social and historical conditions and movements which enable us to speak, with some fullness of
voice, of a human history.[21]

In a realist novel such as *Hard Times* we enter, I claim, that full world of
human effort, that "real substance" of life within which, alone, politics can
speak with a full and fully human voice.[22] This human understanding, based
in part on emotional responses, is the indispensable underpinning of a well-
guided abstract or formal approach.

The Judicious Spectator

So far I have argued only that emotions can sometimes be rational, and that
the emotions of sympathy, fear, and so on, constructed by a literary work
such as *Hard Times* are good candidates for being rational emotions. I have
not yet said very much about which emotions we are to trust or how literary
readership helps us to discriminate the trustworthy from the untrustworthy.
But if we have no reliable filtering device, we might still wonder whether we
should trust emotions at all. I shall now argue that such a device can be
found in Adam Smith's conception of the judicious spectator, and that literary readership (as Smith himself suggests) offers an artificial construction of
the position of such a spectator. It thus supplies a filtering device for emotion
of just the sort that Smith thought necessary for emotions to play the valuable role they ought to play in public life.

We must begin by noting that Adam Smith, in many respects the founder
of modern economics, did not believe that ideal rationality was devoid of
emotion. In fact, he devoted a major part of his career to developing a theory of emotional rationality, since he believed that the guidance of certain
emotions was an essential ingredient in public rationality. In *The Theory of*

Moral Sentiments, he describes a figure whom he calls the "judicious specta-tor," whose judgments and responses are intended to provide a paradigm of public rationality (whether for the leader or for the citizen). The spectator's artificially constructed situation is designed to model the rational moral point of view, by ensuring that he will have those, and only those, thoughts, sentiments, and fantasies that are part of a rational outlook on the world.[23]

The judicious spectator is, first of all, a spectator. That is, he is not person-ally involved in the events he witnesses, although he cares about the partici-pants as a concerned friend. He will not, therefore, have such emotions and thoughts as relate to his own personal safety and happiness; in that sense he is without bias and surveys the scene before him with a certain sort of detachment. He may of course use any information about what is going on that he derives from his own personal history—but this information must be filtered for bias in favor of his own goals and projects. On the other hand, he is not for that reason lacking in feeling. Among his most important moral faculties is the power of imagining vividly what it is like to be each of the persons whose situation he imagines.

> [T]he spectator must . . . endeavour, as much as he can, to put himself in the situation of the other, and to bring home to himself every little circum-stance of distress which can possibly occur to the sufferer. He must adopt the whole case of his companion with all its minutest incidents; and strive to render as perfect as possible, that imaginary change of situation upon which his sympathy is founded. (1.1.4.6)

But sympathetic identification with the parties before him is not sufficient for spectatorial rationality. Smith understands that often the misfortunes that befall the parties damage their ability to assess their own situation cor-rectly. At the most extreme, we may imagine a case in which an accident has caused the person before us to lose the use of reason altogether. If the person's life is painless, empathy might well show us the pleasure of a con-tented child. But, Smith observes, the judicious spectator will nonetheless view the calamity as "of all the calamities to which the condition of mortality exposes mankind . . . by far the most dreadful." What this shows us is that both empathetic participation and external assessment are crucial in de-termining the degree of compassion it is rational to have for the person: "The compassion of the spectator must arise altogether from the consideration of what he himself would feel if he was reduced to the same unhappy situation, and, what is perhaps impossible, was at the same time able to regard it with his present reason and judgment."

Since Smith, a follower of ancient Greek cognitive conceptions of emotion, holds that emotions such as pity, fear, anger, and joy are based on belief and reasoning, he does not hesitate to describe the point of view of the spectator as one rich in emotion. Not only compassion and sympathy, but also fear, grief, anger, hope, and certain types of love are felt by the spectator as a result of his vivid imagining.[24] It would seem bizarre to omit these emotions: Smith's position (like mine) holds that they are entailed by certain thoughts that it is appropriate to have about what is happening to the person before us, and its importance, indeed that they are part of the equipment with which we register what is happening. The spectator's responses are not just willed attitudes of concern, they are really emotions; and Smith plainly believes that the cultivation of appropriate emotions is important for the life of the citizen. Appropriate emotions are useful in showing us what we might do, and also morally valuable in their own right, as recognitions of the character of the situation before us. Furthermore, they motivate appropriate action.

On the other hand, not all emotions are good guides. To be a good guide, the emotion must, first of all, be informed by a true view of what is going on—of the facts of the case, of their significance for the actors in the situation, and of any dimensions of their true significance or importance that may elude or be distorted in the actors' own consciousness. Second, the emotion must be the emotion of a spectator, not a participant. This means not only that we must perform a reflective assessment of the situation to figure out whether the participants have understood it correctly and reacted reasonably; it means, as well, that we must omit that portion of the emotion that derives from our personal interest in our own well-being. The device of the judicious spectator is aimed above all at filtering out that portion of anger, fear, and so on, that focuses on the self. If my friend suffers an injustice, I become angry on his behalf; but, according to Smith, that anger lacks the special vindictive intensity of much anger at wrongs done to oneself. Again, if my friend is grieving for the loss of a loved one, I will share his grief, but not, it appears, its blinding and disabling excess. For Smith, thinking of this distinction helps us to think of what we should be as citizens: passionate for the well-being of others, but not inserting ourselves into the picture that we responsively contemplate.

What we now should notice is that throughout this discussion Smith uses literary readership (and spectatorship at dramas) to illustrate the stance, and the emotions, of the judicious spectator. Smith attaches considerable importance to literature as a source of moral guidance. Its importance derives from the fact that readership is, in effect, an artificial construction of judicious spectatorship, leading us in a pleasing natural way into the attitude that befits the good citizen and judge. As we read we are immersed and intensely concerned participants, yet we lack concrete knowledge of where we are in the scene before us. We care about both Louisa and Stephen Blackpool, to some extent we identify with both, and yet we lack that special and often confused intensity of emotion that would derive from thinking that it is really our own life that is at issue in one or the other case. This also means that we are not prejudicially located: we can feel for both Louisa and Stephen in a more balanced way than can either of them, precisely because we are at the same time both of them and neither. Once again, there are many different readers with different personal histories, and judicious readers are permitted to make use of information about what is going on that derives from their histories. (That is why ideally the process of reading must be completed by a conversation among readers.) But this information, being exercised toward lives that are not ours, will lack the personal bias of the interested participant.

The view of human hopes and fears that the judicious reader forms in the process of reading the novel is not foolproof. As I have said, emotions are good guides only if they are based on a true view of the facts of the case and a true view of the importance of various types of suffering and joy for human actors of many types. (Like other judgments, they must be tested for coherence with our other experiences and with our moral and political theories.) It is obvious that literary works can distort the world for their readers in these two ways. They can present historical and scientific fact falsely, as Dickens to a great extent falsely depicts the labor union movement, and as many novelists present a distorted picture of the capacities of women or of religious and racial minorities. They can also misrepresent the importance of various types of suffering or harm, leading us to think them either graver or lighter than they really are. Thus Dickens suggests that workers will flourish if only they are diverted and given some leisure time; he does not rate high enough the harm involved in class hierarchy itself. Dickens also fails to take note of harms caused to women by inequalities of autonomy that are endemic to marriage as it was lived in his time. I shall argue in the next chapter, as I have already suggested in the previous one, that there are aspects of the imagination of the reader that lead toward social equality rather than its opposite, that tend to detect and undermine hierarchies of race and class and gender. But one must concede that this tendency is not universally practiced, and to this extent novels (like any other text) will offer a guidance that is, if promising, still fallible and incomplete.

This shows us that we need to exercise critical judgment in our selection of novels, and to continue the process of critical judgment as we read, in dialogue with other readers. Wayne Booth has aptly called this process "co-duction," since it is by its nature a nondeductive, comparative type of practical reasoning that is carried on in cooperation with others. In the process of co-duction, our intuitions about a literary work will be refined by the criticisms of ethical theory and of friendly advice, and this may greatly alter the emotional experience that we are able to have as readers—if, for example, we find ourselves convinced that the novel's invitations to anger and disgust and love are based on a view of the world we can no longer share.

In short, my view does not urge a naive uncritical reliance on the literary work.[25] I have insisted that the conclusions we are apt to draw on the basis of our literary experience need the continued critical scrutiny of moral and political thought, of our own moral and political intuitions, and of the judgments of others. I have, however, argued, with Smith, that the formal structures implicit in the experience of literary readership give us a kind of guidance that is indispensable to any further inquiry—including a critical inquiry about the literary work itself. If we do not begin with "fancy" and wonder about the human shapes before us, with sympathy for their sufferings and joy at their well-being, if we do not appreciate the importance of viewing each person as separate with a single life to live, then our critique of pernicious emotions will have little basis. Readership, as I have argued, gives us this basis—and it also gives us the stance of judicious spectatorship essential to the critique. The reader of *Hard Times* is well placed to begin a critique of the novel's picture of the happiness of workers, wellplaced by the structures of attention and sympathy inherent in the act of reading itself.

The reader cultivates concern with human agency and autonomy and, at the same time, a capacity to imagine what the life of a worker such as Stephen Blackpool is like. This combination is likely to engender in Dickens's readers a dissatisfaction with Dickens's own somewhat glib and condescending solution. Thus one does not need to think the politics of a novel correct in all ways to find the experience itself politically valuable.

I now return to the California jury. The judicious spectator/reader learns an emotional repertory that is rich and intense but free from the special bias that derives from knowing one's own personal stake in the outcome. A reader's emotions will also be constrained by the "record"—by the fact that they are restricted to the information presented in the text. In this way, we can now see, the judicious spectator is an extremely good model for the juror. The juror, of course, is not simply the judicious spectator. Jurors will be constrained in specifically legal ways in what they may consider, not only by the restrictions on bias already built into Smith's model. All the same, keeping Smith's requirements in mind should help us to sort out some of the complex issues involved in the discussion of relevant and irrelevant juror sympathy.

All the opinions in *California v. Brown* agreed that a jury at the penalty phase should ignore only "the sort of sympathy that was not rooted in the aggravating and mitigating evidence introduced during the penalty phase."[26] "Extraneous emotion" was indeed to be disregarded, but emotion appropriately grounded in the evidence was not. An earlier case, *Woodson v. North Carolina,* had set out the importance of such sympathetic emotion in an eloquent way, insisting on the connection between sympathy and being treated as a unique person with one's own narrative history:

> A process that accords no significance to relevant facets of the character and record of the individual offender or the circumstances of the particular offense excludes from consideration in fixing the ultimate punishment of death the possibility of compassionate or mitigating factors stemming from the diverse frailties of humankind. It treats all persons convicted of a designated offense not as uniquely individual human beings, but as members of a faceless, undifferentiated mass to be subjected to the blind infliction of the penalty of death.[27]

All the opinions in *California v. Brown* acknowledge this precedent, thus validating the role of the norm of judicious spectatorship, and also its connection with following the entirety of a complex narrative history. They differ only about whether the instruction as stated (which asks jurors to disregard "mere" sympathy) would naturally be interpreted to demand the exclusion of appropriate sympathy. The majority opinion holds that jurors would readily see that they were being asked only to disregard "untethered" sympathy, while the dissenters argue that the jurors would not be clear about this, given the way in which prosecutors standardly represent the instruction. My argument indicates that the dissenters are correct: there is great confusion in many people's thought on this point, and a corresponding need to clarify the boundaries of appropriate and inappropriate sympathy. Sympathetic emotion that is tethered to the evidence, institutionally constrained in appropriate ways, and free from reference to one's own situation appears to be not only acceptable but actually essential to public judgment. But it is this sort of emotion, the emotion of the judicious spectator, that literary works construct in their readers, who learn what it is to have emotion, not for a "faceless undifferentiated mass," but for the "uniquely individual human being." This means, I believe, that literary works are what Smith thought they were: artificial constructions of some crucial elements in a norm of public rationality, and valuable guides to correct response.

4

Poets as Judges

I read something that moved me a lot not very long ago. I was reading something by Chesterton, and he was talking about one of the Brontës, I think her Jane Eyre. He says you go and look out at the city — I think he was looking at London — and he said you know, you see all those houses now, even at the end of the nineteenth century, and they look all as if they're the same. And you think all those people are out there going to work and they're all the same. He says, but what Brontë tells you is they're not the same. Each one of those persons in each one of those houses and each one of those families is different, and they each have a story to tell. Each of those stories involves something about human passion. Each of those stories involves a man, a woman, children, families, work, lives — and you get that sense out of the book. And so sometimes I've found literature very helpful as a way out of the tower.

Stephen G. Breyer, to Senate Judiciary Committee in
hearings on his nomination to the U.S. Supreme Court

By telling prisoners that no aspect of their individuality, from a photo of a child to a letter from a wife, is entitled to constitutional protection, the Court breaks with the ethical tradition that I had thought was enshrined forever in our jurisprudence.

Justice Stevens, *Hudson v. Palmer,* 1984

The Arbiter of the Diverse

In 1867, standing "by blue Ontario's shore," Walt Whitman "mused of these warlike days and of peace return'd, and the dead that return no more."

And as he mused, a "Phantom gigantic superb, with stern visage, accosted" him, demanding poets for the public life of America. This Phantom—the fused presence, I think, of the young war dead and their dead president— claims that only poets are fully equipped to embody norms of judgment that will hold these states together as a nation. "Their Presidents," comments the Phantom, "shall not be their common referee so much as their poets shall."

The Phantom goes on to describe the poet as a certain sort of judge. But this poet-judge embodies a very particular norm of judgment, one that sets him at odds with many of the conventional models of judging that Whitman finds prevalent on the public scene. Here is part of the Phantom's norma- tive description:

> Of these states the poet is the equable man,
> Not in him but off from him things are grotesque, eccentric, fail of their
>   full returns . . .
> He bestows on every object or quality its fit proportion, neither more nor
>   less,
> He is the arbiter of the diverse, he is the key,
> He is the equalizer of his age and land, . . .
> The years straying toward infidelity he witholds by his steady faith,
> He is no arguer, he is judgment (Nature accepts him absolutely,)
> He judges not as the judge judges but as the sun falling round a helpless
>   thing . . .
> He sees eternity in men and women, he does not see men and women as
>   dreams or dots.

Whitman calls the poet-judge "the equable man," thus setting his ideal in a tradition of thought about legal and judicial reasoning that stretches directly back to Aristotle, who developed a normative conception of equit- able judgment to take the place of an excessively simple or reductive reliance on abstract general principles. Whitman, like Aristotle, claims that this flex- ible context-specific judging is not a concession to the irrational, but the most complete expression of the politically rational: not "in him" but "off from him" things "are grotesque, eccentric, fail of their full returns." The poet is no capricious whimsical creature, but the person best equipped to "bestow on every object or quality its fit proportion," duly weighing the claims of a diverse population, with his gaze fixed both on norms of fairness ("he is the equalizer of his age and land") and also on history ("the years straying toward infidelity he witholds by his steady faith"). Both fairness and history are always to some extent at risk in democracy; the poet-judge is their protector.

Whitman's Phantom now says some obscure and apparently contradictory things about the poet for whom he longs. First, "he is no arguer, he is judgment"; then, "he judges not as the judge judges but as the sun falling round a helpless thing." Why is the poet not an "arguer," but "judgment"? How can he *be* judgment, if he does not judge "as the judge judges"? And what mode of judging is suggested in the strange metaphor of light?

I suggest that the key to these puzzling lines is contained in the later line in which the poet "sees eternity in men and women, he does not see men and women as dreams or dots." Here the contrast is between an abstract pseudomathematical vision of human beings and a rich and concrete vision that does justice to human lives. This, I think, is also the way to read the contrast between being an "arguer" and being "judgment": the poet does not merely present abstract formal considerations, he presents equitable judgments, judgments that fit the historical and human complexities of the particular case. This, the Phantom now goes on to point out, is not the way of most current judges: thus the poet does not judge "as the judge judges." We can best get an idea of what his procedure *is* like, he suggests, by thinking of the way sunlight falls around a "helpless thing." This bold image suggests, first, enormous detail and particularity. When the sun falls around a thing it illuminates every curve, every nook; nothing remains hidden, nothing unperceived. So, too, does the poet's judgment fall, perceiving all that is there and disclosing it to our view. (The image is thus similar to Aristotle's image of the architect's flexible ruler that bends to suit the shape of the stone.)[1] In particular, the sun illuminates the situation of the helpless, which is usually shrouded in darkness. But this intimacy is also stern and rather pitiless: by comparing judgment to sunlight rather than gentle shade, Whitman indicates that the poet's commitment to fairness and fitness does not yield to bias or favor, that his confrontation with the particular, while intimate, is unswerving. There is a certain ideal of judicial neutrality here—a neutrality, however, linked not with remote generality but with rich historical concreteness, not with quasi-scientific abstractness but with a vision of the human world.

All of this is a description of judgment. It is also a description of the literary imagination. It is Whitman's startling claim that the literary imagination should play an important role in supplying "these States" with norms of legal and, especially, judicial reasoning, through an Aristotelian conception of practical judgment. In this chapter, I shall defend that claim. I shall not accept Whitman's claim without qualification, for I shall insist that technical legal reasoning, knowledge of law, and the constraints of precedent play a central role in good judging, suppling the bounds within which the imagination must work. The judge cannot be simply a poet, or even simply an Aristotelian equitable man. Whitman neglects the institutional constraints on the judge's role, treating him as free to follow his own fancy, and this is surely wrong. But I shall argue that, properly restricted, the sort of imagining I have described in chapters 2 and 3 can often supplement the other aspects of judicial reasoning in a valuable way. I shall argue the literary/Aristotelian conception, combined with institutional constraints, yields a complex ideal of judicial neutrality that is a powerful rival to other influential conceptions of that norm.

In particular, I shall contrast the literary judge with three rivals: a judge who cultivates skeptical detachment, a judge who conceives of judicial reasoning on the model of formal reasoning in the sciences, and a judge who cultivates a lofty distance from particulars for reasons of judicial neutrality. I shall argue that the literary judge has good reasons for eschewing skeptical detachment and for preferring to quasi-scientific models an evaluative humanistic form of practical reasoning; these reasons are deeply rooted in the common-law tradition. She does pursue neutrality, but in a manner that coheres with our account of the judicious spectator in chapter 3, requiring, rather than forbidding, sympathetic knowledge of value-laden human facts.

Turning next to Whitman's claim that the poet is "the equalizer of his age and land," I shall develop the connection between the experience of the literary imaginer and a concern with social equality. Finally, I shall examine some judicial opinions that give both good and bad examples of the kind of judging Whitman recommends.

It must be borne in mind that I consider the specifically literary aspects of my "literary judge" to be just one aspect of the thinking of a real-life judge. The real-life judge must also have other abilities and knowledge and is constrained in many ways by her institutional role and by the demands of statute and precedent, which already establish what she may and may not consider salient. The literary aspects of judging can most easily be incorporated into an understanding of judicial reasoning that derives from the common-law tradition, with its already Aristotelian emphasis on the particular. But that tradition does not permit a judge to exercise untethered sympathy or fancy. We must ask, then, how fancy operates within the strict confines of a formal judicial role.

Neither Skepticism nor Scientism

When we read a novel such as *Hard Times,* reading not as literary theorists asking about theories of interpretation, but as human beings who are moved and delighted, we are, I have argued, judicious spectators, free from personal bias and favor. At the same time, we are clearly not skeptics. We do not all react in exactly the same way to the characters and their situation. But the structure of the novel—its ways of presenting the world to us and its enticements to identify ourselves with certain characters rather than others—set us up, if we respond to them, in a posture of the heart and mind that is not one of skeptical indifference, that does not feel that anything at all that happens to these people is as good as every other thing. We can, of course, withhold ourselves from the novel's invitation to engage ourselves with it in the ways it suggests (though then it is not evident why we would continue to read). But if we follow the story with eager attention, succumbing to its invitations and being moved by its people, then we are, in the process, making judgments—about the industrial revolution, about utilitarianism, about divorce law, about the education of children—confident in the process that some reasons are indeed stronger than others, that some ways of treating human beings are themselves better than others and can be justified as better by the giving of such reasons.

We are, in effect, being constituted by the novel as judges of a certain sort. As judges we may dispute with one another about what is right and proper; but insofar as the characters matter to us, and we are active on their behalf, we do not feel that the dispute is about nothing at all that we are merely playing around. Such judgments (for example, our judgments about the moral education of Louisa Gradgrind, and of children more generally) are usually not based on transcendent extrahistorical standards. Indeed, our experience as readers leads us to think that such standards would be unnecessary for our search, for as concerned readers we search for a human good that we are trying to bring about in and for the human community, and it is not evident why norms external to the experience of human striving should be required for such a project. Our search is guided, as well, by the judgments and responses of our fellow readers, who themselves are seeking such a comprehensive fit. What we are after is not just a view of moral education that makes sense of our own personal experience, but one that we can defend to others and support along with others with whom we wish to live in community. This, too, anchors our reading and makes it fundamentally different from the free play of interpretive faculties.[2]

It is important to emphasize the nonskeptical character of ordinary reading, since a highly skeptical approach to legal reasoning has recently been defended from within literary theory, using the activity of literary interpreting as an alleged paradigm. Stanley Fish, perhaps the leading proponent of this sort of view in the law, holds that without standards that transcend history and human interpretive activity—which he thinks we have failed to find—we are left with the play of political and historical forces which cause us to believe certain things but which can give no principled justifications for those beliefs.[3] In other words, take away extrahistorical justification and you do away with all rational justification. You are left with causes but no good reasons.[4] But this leap—as it were, from the heavens to the abyss—is not entailed by any argument that Fish has presented or that can easily be imagined. Even if it should be shown that we lack extrahistorical standards for public and legal reasoning, this should not disturb us very much, for the law has always based its reasoning on history and social context and has rarely attached importance to establishing an eternal basis for its judgments. Fish has not shown, nor could he, I think, show that within the tradition of human reasoning about ethics and law we cannot single out some arguments as stronger than others, some positions as more defensible than others. The experience of the reader of literature shows how we do this: by bringing our evolving sense of principle and tradition to bear on a concrete context. Fish arrives at detachment from normative argument only by setting the goal of argument so unreasonably high that it can never be met by human beings. In real life, however, we set more modest goals, and frequently we meet them. If this is so in ethical reasoning generally, it is all the more clearly so in the law, for the system of precedent and legal constraint contribute to the defeat of indeterminacy, even more powerfully, perhaps, than the moral imagination itself.

If the literary view strongly repudiates detachment from good reasons, it also repudiates the idea that the law can or should be understood on the model of natural science. The scientistic view keeps on appearing, in various forms, throughout the history of Anglo-American law, primarily as an attack on what appears to be the messy, unsystematic character of the common-law tradition. In a revealing autobiographical passage, Benjamin Cardozo compares the hope for a scientific system to a quest for paradise, for something different from the human world that we actually inhabit:

> I was much troubled in spirit, in my first years upon the bench, to find how trackless was the ocean on which I had embarked. I sought for certainty. I was oppressed and disheartened when I found that the quest for it was futile. I was trying to reach land, the solid land of fixed and settled rules, the paradise of a justice that would declare itself by tokens plainer and more commanding than its pale and glimmering reflections in my own vacillating mind and conscience. I found with the voyagers in Browning's "Paracelsus" that "the real heaven was always beyond."[5]

One can see how someone who clings to that ideal (as Cardozo did not) could easily fall into Fish-style detachment out of discouragement at failures to attain it. Such a conclusion would betray, however, a kind of shame about the historically grounded and yet principled reasons that the law actually uses.

One can see a similar repudiation of practical reason in Christopher Columbus Langdell, founder of the modern conception of legal education, who argued that the law would have a place in a great university such as Harvard only if it could justify its claim to be a science. "If it be not a science," he wrote, "it is a species of handicraft, and may best be learned by serving an apprenticeship to one who practises it." To Langdell, showing that law was a science required showing that it was constituted by a Platonic hierarchy of simple and general principles that were fixed in advance of cases (though built up in the first place by examining cases), and that would yield an almost mechanical decision procedure: "The true lawyer is one who has such a mastery of legal principles as to be able to apply them with constant facility and certainty to the ever-tangled skein of human affairs."[6] In more recent times, the scientific aspiration has been focused on the assimilation of law to the science of economics—an idea some of whose application I have criticized in chapters 2 and 3.

The idea that the law is a respectable academic field only if it is a science in one of these senses ignores an obvious possibility: that the law is a humanistic as well as a scientific field, and that its excellences include the special excellences of practical reasoning as they are understood in the humanities. As Aristotle long ago argued, reasoning in ethics and politics is and ought to be different from the deductive reasoning some seek in the sciences, for it must be concerned in a more fundamental way with historical change, with the complexity of actual practical contexts, and with the sheer diversity of cases. For all of these reasons, though it will certainly seek and use rules as guides, it will also attend to the details of cases and will not simply assume in advance that the rule as stated antecedently will be fully adequate to cover the cases. Although fixed rules have a very important place to play in legal judgment—for example, in ensuring stability, in preventing bias, and in reducing errors of judgment, legal judgments must also accommodate changing circumstances and changing values, confronting the case that is actually at hand.[7] Aristotle's norm of practical reason is well exemplified in the characteristic procedures of the common law, with its rich attention to history and circumstance.

Judicial Neutrality

The literary judge—like Whitman's beam of sunlight—is committed to neutrality, properly understood. That is, she will not tailor her principles to the demands of political or religious pressure groups and will give no group or individual special indulgence or favor on account of their relation to her or her affiliations. She is a judicious spectator and does not gush with irrelevant or ungrounded sentiment. On the other hand, as I have argued here, her neutrality does not require a lofty distance from the social realities of the cases before her; indeed, she is enjoined to examine those realities searchingly, with imaginative concreteness and the emotional responses that are proper to the judicious spectator—or to his surrogate, the novel-reader. In chapter 2, I suggested that the literary judge would look in particular for evidence that certain groups have suffered unequal disadvantages and therefore need more attention if they are to be shown a truly equal concern.

This concern for the disadvantaged is built into the structure of the literary experience, which was, as we saw, Adam Smith's model for the experience of the judicious spectator. The reader participates vicariously in numerous different lives, some more advantaged and some less. In realist social novels, which are my focus, these lives are self-consciously drawn from different social strata, and the extent to which these varied circumstances allow for flourishing is made part of the reader's experience. The reader enters each of these lives not knowing, so to speak, which one of them is hers—she identifies first with Louisa and then with Stephen Blackpool, living each of those lives in turn and becoming aware that her actual place is in many respects an accident of fortune. She has empathetic emotions appropriate to the living of the life and, more important, spectatorial emotions in which she evaluates the way fortune has made this life conducive or not conducive to flourishing. This means, as I argue in the next section, that she will notice especially vividly the disadvantages faced by the least well off. In the case of Dickens's novel, for example, she is likely to feel that Stephen Blackpool, given the disadvantages under which he labors, requires a special degree of attention if he is to be shown a truly equal concern as a citizen.

This conception of the spectator goes to the heart of the famous and controversial argument of Herbert Wechsler in "Toward Neutral Principles of Constitutional Law."[8] The literary judge strongly agrees with the general view of judgment articulated by Wechsler near the beginning of the article: judges need criteria that are not arbitrary or capricious, "criteria that can be framed and tested as an exercise of reason and not merely as an act of willfulness or will." A good decision is indeed one "that rests on reasons with respect to all the issues in the case, reasons that in their generality and their neutrality transcend any immediate result that is involved." The reasons should meet a standard of public articulability and principled consistency. We should strongly resist the idea that the courts do or should operate as a "naked power organ." It is in fact a similar idea of neutrality and freedom from situational bias that motivates Smith's construction of the judicious spectator, through the device of thinking about the reader of narrative fiction. Where legal reasoning is concerned, we need to add to Smith's model the fact that there will also be powerful institutional constraints on the

judge's reasoning, and this will give us yet further reasons to agree with
Wechsler in his demand for principled neutrality.

As his argument continues, however, Wechsler turns sharply away from
the Smith ideal of neutrality to a more remote and abstract norm. He seems
to understand neutrality to demand that one stand so far away from present
circumstances and their history that one will ignore many specific social and
historical facts—facts that seem highly relevant to the equal and principled
application of the law. Although in the theoretical part of the article he does
insist that his conception of principle does not entail disregarding history
and legal precedent, in his reading of the school-desegregation cases, he
appears to disregard some highly pertinent social data in the name of stick-
ing to "the facts." In particular, he suggests that judges deciding cases relating to "separate but equal" facilities should refuse themselves concrete empathetic knowledge of the special disadvantages faced by minorities and the
asymmetrical meaning of segregation for blacks and whites, in order to ensure that their principles are applied without political bias:

> [T]he separate-but-equal formula was not overruled "in form" but was held
> to have "no place" in public education on the ground that segregated
> schools are "inherently unequal," with deleterious effects upon the colored
> children in implying their inferiority, effects which retard their educational
> and mental development. . . .
>
> I find it hard to think the judgment really turned upon the facts. Rather,
> it seems to me, it must have rested on the view that racial segregation is, in
> principle, a denial of equality to the minority against whom it is di-
> rected. . . . But this position also presents problems. . . . In the context of a
> charge that segregation *with equal facilities* is a denial of equality, is there not
> a point in *Plessy* in the statement that if "enforced separation stamps the
> colored race with a badge of inferiority" it is solely because its members
> choose "to put that construction upon it"? Does enforced separation of the
> sexes discriminate against females merely because it may be the females
> who resent it and it is imposed by judgments predominantly male? Is a
> prohibition of miscegenation a discrimination against the colored member
> of the couple who would like to marry?
>
> For me, assuming equal facilities, the question posed by state-enforced
> segregation is not one of discrimination at all. Its human and its constitu-
> tional dimensions lie entirely elsewhere, in the denial by the state of free-

dom to associate, a denial that impinges in the same way on any groups or races that may be involved. . . . In the days when I was joined with Charles H. Houston in a litigation in the Supreme Court, before the present building was constructed, he did not suffer more than I in knowing that we had to go to Union Station to lunch together during the recess.

Wechsler claims, notice, to state not only the constitutional but also the "human" meaning of the laws in question. He is wrong on both counts. There is such a lofty distance from the human facts of the matter that the principles are not correct. Had Wechsler imagined the lunch incident in the manner of a novelist, considering the meaning, for Houston, of knowing that he could not lunch with Wechsler at a downtown restaurant, he would quickly have seen that the meaning of that denial of the freedom to associate is strongly asymmetrical—for Wechsler, an inconvenience and (as he elsewhere notes) a source of guilt; for Houston, a public brand of inferiority. One cannot consider the history of race relations in this country closely and sympathetically, in the manner of Smith's judicious spectator, without noticing this asymmetry. Wechsler's claim that the issue is not one of discrimination at all has about it a bizarre sort of Martian neutrality. From his enforced distance from the emotions involved in the experience of oppression, he fails to notice perfectly reasonable and universalizable principles that do include the asymmetrical meaning of segregation and the history of segregation as stigma. These notions are highly relevant to the interpretation of the Constitution, and to the formulation of appropriate constitutional, as well as human, principles. Wechsler's failure of imagination is equally evident in the gender example, which, it would seem, is intended to serve as a *reductio ad absurdum* of his racial point: if separate-but-equal is wrong for race, it must be wrong for gender. But we know that people who complain about gender-separation are women who are complaining on account of a political agenda, not on account of reasons that can be articulated in a principled way. This seems to be the message of his argument. Once again, however, there are many ways in which the historical asymmetry between men and women can be made the subject of principled argument, argument that rests on reasons and is not simply tailored to achieve a particular result.

The literary judge, by contrast, holds that such social and historical facts are relevant, and that the judge in such a case should develop as rich and comprehensive an understanding as possible of the situation of the groups involved in the case. She should not be swayed by any personal connection or any partisan goal. Her emotions should be those of the judicious spectator, not personal emotions bearing on her own profit or loss in the case at hand, or any other personal taste or goal that is grounded in her own situation rather than the situation of which she is the spectator. They should not simply be the emotions of the actors involved, though empathy with the actors will usually be one important part of the process of judicious spectatorship, through which the judge takes the measure of the suffering of the people. The judicious spectator must go beyond empathy, assessing from her own spectatorial viewpoint the meaning of those sufferings and their implications for the lives involved. People can be wrong about what is happening to them in many ways. As spectators, we may find that Stephen Blackpool exaggerates the wrong done to him by society, or we may find— as I think we really do when we read Dickens—that his political deprivations have made him if anything too well adapted to his misery, too ready to accept a small relief rather than demanding full equality. So detached evaluation is at the heart of the activity of the literary imaginer as judicious spectator. But this does not mean being ignorant of, or refusing to acknowledge, sufferings and inequities that are all too much a part of history. Literary neutrality, like Whitman's sunlight, like the reading of a novel, gets close to the people and their actual experience. That is how it is able to be fair and to perform its own detached evaluation correctly.

The Equalizer of His Age and Land

Whitman calls his poet-judge an "equalizer." What does he mean? Why should the literary imagination be any more connected with equality than with inequality, or with democratic rather than aristocratic ideals? Why is the sunlight of judicial vision specially concerned with the "helpless thing"?

When we read *Hard Times* as sympathetic participants, our attention has a special focus. Since the sufferings and anxieties of the characters are among the central bonds between reader and work, our attention is drawn in particular to those characters who suffer and fear. Characters who are not facing any adversity simply do not hook us in as readers; there is no drama in a life in which things are going smoothly. This tragic sensibility leads the reader to investigate with a particularly keen combination of identification and sympathy lives in which circumstance has played an impeding role. Sometimes, of course, the baneful circumstances are necessary and inevitable. Loved ones die; natural disasters destroy property and cities. Frequently, however, the tragedy that moves us is not necessary. Not all wars are inevitable; hunger and poverty and miserably unequal conditions of labor are not inevitable. Since we read a novel like *Hard Times* with the thought that we ourselves might be in a character's position—since our emotion is based in part on this sort of empathetic identification—we will naturally be most concerned with the lot of those whose position is worst, and we will begin to think of ways in which that position might have been other than it is, might be made better than it is.

One way in which the situation of the poor or oppressed is especially bad is that it might have been otherwise. We see this especially clearly when we see their situation side by side with the situation of the rich and prosperous. In this way our thought will naturally turn in the direction of making the lot of the worst off more similar to the lot of the rich and powerful: since we ourselves might be, or become, either of those two people, we want to raise the floor. This may not get all the way to complete equality (whether of resources or of welfare or of capability to function), but it does at least lead political thought in the direction of ameliorating persistent inequalities and providing all with a decent minimum. One might of course have these thoughts without being a "poet." But it is Whitman's point, I think, that the ability to imagine vividly, and then to assess judicially, another person's pain, to participate in it and then to ask about its significance, is a powerful way of learning what the human facts are and of acquiring a motivation to alter them. If one could not imagine what it was like to be Stephen Blackpool, then it would be all too easy to neglect his situation as Bounderby does, portraying workers as grasping insensitive beings. Similarly, to take a case that will figure in my next section, if one cannot imagine what women suffer from sexual harassment on the job, one won't have a vivid sense of that offense as a serious social infringement that the law should remedy. In neither case does the judicious spectator stop with the experience of the other person's pain: one must then ask, from the spectatorial viewpoint, whether that pain is appropriate to its target, whether it is such pain, or anger, or fear, as a reasonable person would feel in those circumstances. But the sense of what was really experienced is a crucial step along the way, without which any spectatorial assessment may miss the mark.

The literary judge is also an equalizer in another closely related way. I have argued that the experience of novel-reading yields a strong commitment to regard each life as individual and separate from other lives. This way of seeing things is highly relevant to the questions of well-being I have just addressed: Stephen's misery is not bought off by Bounderby's exceeding good fortune. But it has another kind of relevance as well. Group hatred and the oppression of groups is very often based on a failure to individualize. Racism, sexism, and many other forms of pernicious prejudice frequently ground themselves in the attribution of negative characteristics to the entire group. Sometimes—as in the case of the Nazi depiction of Jews, as in the case of much of the "thinking" characteristic of American racism—this is carried to the extreme of portraying the group as altogether subhuman, as vermin, insects, even as "cargo," an attitude that cannot survive the individualized knowledge of a member or members of that group. This does not mean that even in contact with an individual one cannot find many ways of dehumanizing him or her in thought. It means, however, that when one does manage for whatever reason to take up to the individual the literary attitude of sympathetic imagining, the dehumanizing portrayal is unsustainable, at least for a time.[9] A memorable moment of this kind is the scene in the film *Schindler's List,* in which the German camp commandant holds his Jewish housemaid by the chin, as she stands terrified in her slip, and asks, torn between dogma and personal desire, "Is this the face of a rat?"

Literary understanding, I would therefore argue, promotes habits of mind that lead toward social equality in that they contribute to the dismantling of the stereotypes that support group hatred. For this purpose, in principle any literary work that has the characteristics I have discussed in chapter 1 would be valuable: in reading Dickens, we learn habits of "fancying" that we can then apply to other groups that come before us, whether or not those groups are depicted in the novels we have read. But it is also very valuable to extend this literary understanding by seeking out literary experiences in which we do identify sympathetically with individual members of marginalized or oppressed groups within our own society, learning both to see the world, for a time, through their eyes and then reflecting as spectators on the meaning of what we have seen. If one of the significant contributions of the novel to public rationality is its depiction of the interaction between shared human aspirations and concrete social circumstances, it seems reasonable that we should seek novels that depict the special circumstances of groups with whom we live and whom we want to understand, cultivating the habit of seeing the fulfillment or frustration of their aspirations and desires within a social world that may be characterized by institutional inequalities.

One such novel is Richard Wright's *Native Son*. As I taught this novel to an almost entirely white group of law students in the very place where the novel is set, we recognized that most of us were, in effect, in the position of the novel's Mary Dalton, well-meaning but grossly ignorant and undeveloped in sympathy, desirous of knowing what it is like to live the other side of "the line," but unable or unwilling to carry that desire into action. The experience of reading and discussing the novel at least begins to give white readers a knowledge of their ignorance, and to introduce habits of "fancying" that it is crucial to develop if we are to deliberate well about race.

Wright's novel is "equalizing" in both of the ways that I have mentioned—drawing attention to misery and focusing our attention on the individual. From the first, we see the world through the eyes of a particular person who encounters special and terrible disadvantages. We enter a squalid one-room tenement, where Bigger Thomas lives with his mother, his sister, and his brother. "Light flooded the room and revealed a black boy standing in a narrow space between two iron beds."[10] Bigger, seen by the sun—an image that strikingly recalls Whitman's sun "falling round a helpless thing"—is in prison already. Like the rat he shortly kills, he is trapped in a condition of helplessness. We see what it is to try to maintain self-respect and order when you have no privacy to change your clothes, when your pathetic "conspiracy against shame" can be interrupted at any time by a rat running across the floor. We note the way in which the rat, cornered, strikes viciously back, and we sense from then on what Bigger's relation to the world around him will be. In short, as we follow the world to some extent through Bigger's eyes, to some extent as onlookers, we see how at every point his hopes and fears, his sexual longings, his sense of himself, are conditioned by the squalor in which he lives.

Not only squalor. The predominant force in Bigger's self-conception and in his emotional life is racial inequality and hatred. He is aware of himself in images drawn from the white world's denigration of him; he defines himself as worthless because they have defined him in that way. And, like the rat, he strikes back, attempting to use violence as an escape from help-lessness and shame. The novel avoids evoking an easy sympathy that would say, despite differences in circumstance, we are all brothers under the skin. The white reader has difficulty identifying with Bigger; not only his external circumstances, but also his emotions and desires, are the products of social and historical factors. But beneath the facile kind of sympathy lies the possi-bility of a deeper sympathy, one that says: This is a human being, with the basic equipment to lead a productive life; see how not only the external circumstances of action, but also anger, fear, and desire have been deformed by racial hatred and its institutional expression. The unlikeness that repels identification becomes the chief object of our concern.

The reader's experience here shows very clearly what role empathy does and does not play in the activity of the judicious spectator. We cannot follow the novel without trying to see the world through Bigger's eyes. As we do so, we take on, to at least some extent, his emotions of rage and shame. On the other hand, we are also spectators. As spectators we recognize the inappro-priateness of some of his emotions to their object—for example, of his shame at the color of his skin, and of his tragic combination of longing and fear toward the white family. These emotions are all too plausible given his situation, and yet the novel shows their cruel and arbitrary social basis. This leads us as spectators to feel a further range of emotions   a deep sympathy, as I have suggested, for Bigger's predicament, a principled anger at the structures of racism that have made him as he is.

"He knew as he stood there that he could never tell why he had killed. It was not that he did not really want to tell, but the telling of it would have involved an explanation of his entire life." As "judicious spectator" of Big-ger's story, the reader—unlike almost all of the characters—attends to the explanation of his entire life, and comes to an understanding of the genesis of his violent character. The novel suggests that this understanding is essen-tial to the just determination of Bigger's crime and punishment. It thus takes up the position that I discussed in chapter 3 in connection with jury deliber-ation: the criminal must be seen as an individual with a story of his own to tell. This stance does not determine any particular outcome—although, as both *Woodson* and *California v. Brown* suggest, it is frequently connected with mercy in sentencing. Many other issues must be taken into account by both judges and jurors, many of them technical in character. Even the constraints built into the ideal of judicious spectatorship need to be further constrained by specifically legal requirements. But the reader, while judging Bigger culpable (the degree of his culpability is certainly debatable), is likely to be, other things equal, inclined to mercy in the imposition of punishment, seeing how much of his character was the product of circumstances created by others.[11]

What the narrative shows us, however, is that the world in which Bigger Thomas actually lives—with its institutional and legal barriers to mobility, with its racial estrangement and mutual fear and hate—this world, unlike the world of novel-reading, makes the novel-reader's empathetic individualizing stance unavailable across racial lines. Neither Bigger nor the white characters can see members of the other race as distinct individuals, each with their own story to tell. The racial branding of individuals eclipses personal identity. To Bigger, white people are a "mountain of hate." He cannot see them separately, and indeed, the prospect of an individual relationship with Mary Dalton arouses such fear and shame and loathing in him that he is led to the brink of rape and, subsequently, to manslaughter. Mary Dalton attempts to befriend Bigger as an individual, but in a clumsy, ill-judged way in which her perception of him as individual is usually obscured by stereotypes; he is little more to her than a means to rebel against her parents. The novel makes us doubt that any other more personal relationship would have been possible, except in the most unusual circumstances. The legacy of racism thus defeats literary judging, and with it, the hope of friendship and constructive partnership. In this sense the novel, like Dickens's novel, is about itself and recommends itself. Its most powerful charge against America is that its own modes of perception are almost never to be found.

The novel is well known for the speech making of Bigger's lawyer, who, borrowing from Fanon, sees violence as an inevitable response to Bigger's oppression, and perhaps a valuable sort of self-assertion. But it is not on this note that the novel ends, and the lawyer is shown to be just as deaf to Bigger's personal story as many of the other white characters. The novel ends, in fact, with the achievement of sympathy and friendship. During his long imprisonment, Bigger—struck by the courage and decency of Jan, the young communist who has every motive to hate him, but who alone seems to attend to him as a person in his own right—begins to think like a novel-reader. He begins, that is, to think of the deep similarity in human aims and insecurities that may exist on both sides of the racial barrier, though concealed from view by the social deformation of character and desire. At last, in a sudden epiphany, he becomes able to see this common humanity:

> He wondered if it were possible that after all everybody in the world felt alike? Did those who hated him have in them the same thing Max had seen in him, the thing that had made Max ask him those questions? And what motive could Max have in helping? Why would Max risk that white tide of hate to help him? For the first time in his life he had gained a pinnacle of feeling upon which he could stand and see vague relations that he had never dreamed of. If that white looming mountain of hate were not a mountain at all, but people, people like himself, and like Jan—then he was faced with a high hope the like of which he had never thought could be, and a despair the full depths of which he knew he could not stand to feel. . . . He stood up in the middle of the cell floor and tried to see himself in relation to other men, a thing he had always feared to try to do, so deeply stained was his own mind with the hate of others for him.

Racial hatred is a stain and an infection that prevents the individualized, and at the same time the common, view of the humanity of others. (These two perceptions are connected because seeing others as similarly and fully human entails seeing them as individuals with their own stories to tell.) To see white people not as a looming mountain of hate but as people—this is the beginning of hope. But in Bigger's circumstances, as he faces death, it is also despair, for there is, then, a real human life and a human community. He discovers its worth at the same time as he knows his own irrevocable loss of it. The despair encompasses, as well, the knowledge that the forces that have doomed him persist unchanged, that the hope cannot now be realized for anyone, that it will take large-scale institutional and social changes that he cannot even imagine to make that hope a reality for others. His last words are, "Tell Jan hello . . ."—and then "Goodbye!" "He heard the ring of steel against steel as a far door clanged shut."

Engaging the reader in this tragedy of social helplessness, the novel constructs a reader who is a judicious and neutral judge of Bigger Thomas, but a judge whose neutrality is different in kind from Wechsler's and far closer to Whitman's—though constrained, as Whitman's is not, by the specific institutional requirements of the judicial role. The stigma of racial hate and shame emerges as fundamentally deforming of human personality and community, and the novel-reading stance calls out for political and social equality as the necessary condition of full humanity for citizens on both sides of "the line."

To indicate that the connection between literary spectatorship and a concern for equality is not an isolated phenomenon in the case of this novel, let me introduce one further example, which deals with one of the most pressing equality issues of our time. E. M. Forster's *Maurice* was written in 1913–14, but published only in 1971. It could not have been published earlier, its author tells us, because it shows two homosexual lovers ending happily. "Happiness is its keynote. . . . If it ended unhappily, with a lad dangling from a noose or with a suicide pact, all would be well, for there is no pornography or seduction of minors. But the lovers get away unpunished and consequently recommend crime."[12]

The strategy in *Maurice* is to select as hero a man of strong and exclusive homosexual tendencies who is in no other way "unnatural." In fact, he is a boring, snobbish, middle-class English stockbroker of mediocre talent and imagination. The reader is not thrilled by him, but his kindness and his general good nature evoke sympathy. The emotional structure of the novel relies on the ease with which the reader will see Maurice as average, and then see, year by year, how the treatment society accords to his desires—which revolve around rather tender imaginings of a comforting and quasi-marital "friend"—renders him terribly nonaverage and also deeply unequal. From the anatomy lecture on the beach, where the young teacher's quasi-biblical praise of the naturalness of heterosexuality makes the boy feel his own "nature" and impulses to be shameful and deformed, to the Terminal Note, in which Forster reminds us that even in 1971 homosexuals continue to be prosecuted for consensual sexual acts, the novel tells a story of average humanness forced into a situation of repression, fear, and guilt. This inequality is enforced by social prejudices that justify themselves with a language of nature that derives from religious tradition. Readers are led to recognize that Maurice as someone they might know, someone whose desires are not alarming or dangerous. He wants many of the same things heterosexuals want. They also recognize that the desires that lead Maurice to other men are in their own way deeply "natural"—felt in him from an early age in a way he neither chooses nor controls. (The psychiatrist who fails to "cure" him recommends a move to France, saying "England has always been disinclined to accept human nature.") For the person who finds himself to be heterosexual, society gives respect and status; for the person who finds himself to be different, frustration, shame, and continual danger. When Maurice's friend Clive marries a young woman, "[b]eautiful conventions received them—while beyond the barrier Maurice wandered, the wrong words on his lips and the wrong desires in his heart, and his arms full of air."

Though in many ways this novel is extremely distant from *Native Son*—it is set in a sheltered middle-class world, its characters are refined and nonviolent—its common ground is also evident. The image of "the barrier" reminds us of "the line" that separates black from white in Bigger's world. In both cases, there is a division in society that marks some people as normal and good, others as shameful and evil. In both cases, this division brands and stigmatizes the excluded group in ways that are closely connected to systematic inequalities: Maurice may be able to hold a job, but he cannot express his sexual desires openly; he lives continually at risk of prosecution, and he cannot have honest relationships with his friends and fellow workers. In a very real sense, he is not a fully equal citizen. Clive, too, having chosen to forgo homosexual gratification and to enter a passionless marriage, is unequal—for he is forced to lead an essentially dishonest life in a matter of the greatest importance. The novel's last sentence tells us that Clive, having heard of Maurice's affair with Alec, "returned to the house, to correct his proofs and to devise some method of concealing the truth from Anne." Forster notes that Clive and Maurice are as close to equality as they are only because of class advantages that Maurice's lower-class lover lacks. In the Britain of 1971, unless consensual homosexual acts are decriminalized, "Clive on the bench will continue to sentence Alec in the dock. Maurice may get off." In that way, issues of class equality are shown to be linked to the novel's central issue of sexual equality.

The novel, like *Native Son,* like *Hard Times,* refers to itself. Again and again readers notice that they are perceiving Maurice in a very different way from the way of the people around him. Maurice's friends either refuse recognition of his difference or, recognizing it, shun him in horror as if he had suddenly become a monster. They simply cannot permit themselves to imagine for a moment what it may be like to be him. The reader who does imagine is fully aware all along that he is neither the same nor a monster. This means that the reader as judicious spectator is aware in a way the characters are not of the stigmatizing effect of societal prejudice, and of the helplessness it creates. The novel makes its case for equal sexual liberty by showing the profound worth of that liberty in its portraits of the flourishing of Maurice and the stunted life of Clive; and it enlists readers as partisans of that equality by making it easy for them to see Maurice as someone they, or one of their friends or loved ones, might be.

Poetic Judging

My argument in this book is well captured in the quotation from Stephen Breyer's confirmation hearing that I cited as an epigraph to this chapter. The ability to think of people's lives in the novelist's way is, Breyer argues, an important part of the equipment of a judge. A part and not, obviously, the whole, or even the central part—but a vital part nonetheless. This claim is the more impressive in that it comes from a judge who is far from being a sentimentalist, whose technical proficiency is great, and who is, if anything, considered more intellectual than emotional. Even a judge so unsentimental, with such deep technical and intellectual commitments, then, grants that novel-reading is relevant to the judicial imagination. My approach— like, I believe, the approach that Breyer sketches in this statement—stresses the need for technical mastery as well as sentiment and imagination and insists, too, that the latter must continually be informed and tethered by the former.

In order to go further, however, we need examples of judicial opinions that both do and do not manifest the virtues of the literary judge. I have selected two positive examples and one negative.

Hudson v. Palmer, U.S. Supreme Court, 1984.
[Dissenting opinion by Justice Stevens.]

This case was originally brought by Palmer, a prison inmate serving a sentence for forgery, grand larceny, and bank robbery, against Hudson, a police officer who had conducted a shakedown search of his cell.[13] Palmer claimed that the search was conducted solely to harass or humiliate him.[14] Though

claiming to search for contraband, Hudson in the process intentionally destroyed some of Palmer's legitimate personal property—photographs and
letters. Palmer claimed that this destruction of property violated his Fourth
Amendment right against unreasonable searches and seizures, and that the
unauthorized deprivation of property constituted a violation of the proce-
dural due process requirement of the Fourteenth Amendment. In an opinion written by Chief Justice Burger, the majority held that a prison inmate
does not have "a reasonable expectation of privacy in his prison cell entitling
him to the protection of the Fourth Amendment against unreasonable
searches and seizures" (398), and that therefore even the modest notion that
random searches should be conducted within certain established guidelines
(the holding of the Court of Appeals) constrains prison authority too severely: "The recognition of privacy rights for prisoners in their individual
cells simply cannot be reconciled with the concept of incarceration and the
needs and objectives of penal institutions" (403). As for the intentional destruction of property, it does not violate due process given that the state provides "a meaningful postdeprivation remedy" (406).

Justice Stevens (joined by Justices Brennan, Marshall, and Blackmun)
concurs in part and dissents in part. The dissenters agree about the due
process issue, but claim that the Court's reasoning on the Fourth Amendment issue is "seriously flawed," indeed "internally inconsistent" (412–13).
It is inconsistent because the Court grants the possibility of maliciously motivated searches and intentional harassment of prisoners, saying that these
"cannot be tolerated by a civilized society" (413, citing 404), yet maintains
"that no matter how malicious, destructive, or arbitrary a cell search and
seizure may be, it cannot constitute an unreasonable invasion of any privacy
or possessory interest that society is prepared to recognize as reasonable."
The dissenters then spell out the implications of this inconsistency:

> Measured by the conditions that prevail in a free society, neither the posses-
> sions nor the slight residuum of privacy that a prison inmate can retain in
> his cell, can have more than the most minimal value. From the standpoint
> of the prisoner, however, that trivial residuum may mark the difference be-
> tween slavery and humanity. . . . Personal letters, snapshots of family mem-
> bers, a souvenir, a deck of cards, a hobby kit, perhaps a diary or a training
> manual for an apprentice in a new trade, or even a Bible—a variety of
> inexpensive items may enable a prisoner to maintain contact with some

part of his past and an eye to the possibility of a better future. Are all of
these items subject to unrestrained perusal, confiscation, or mutilation at
the hands of a possibly hostile guard? (413)

Stevens now continues with a legal argument. He first distinguishes between Palmer's privacy interest in his property and his possessory interest.[15]
While he does not accept the Court's general rule that a prisoner can have
no expectation of privacy in his papers or effects, he is willing to assume it for
the purposes of the argument. He then argues that the Fourth Amendment
protects Palmer's possessory interest in the property, citing definitions of
"search" and "seizure" in previous cases. He points out that Palmer's posses-
sion of the destroyed material was entirely legitimate as a matter of state law;
therefore the Court is wrong in concluding that, as a prisoner, he could have
no legitimate possessory interests. He points out that in its treatment of Palmer's due process claim the Court itself grants that the destroyed material was
"property" within the meaning of the due process clause, and this entails that
Palmer's claim to the material is a legitimate claim of entitlement (415–16).[16]

Hudson's actions, then, constituted a "seizure." Was the seizure "unreasonable"? This issue can only be resolved by "balancing the intrusion on
constitutionally protected interests against the law enforcement interests jus-
tifying the challenged conduct" (417). Stevens argues that there is no legitimate penological justification for the seizure here. There is no contention
that the property was contraband or posed any risk to institutional security.
Hudson had already examined it before he took it and destroyed it. No motive but spite has been suggested for his conduct. Since the Court itself has
acknowledged that the intentional harassment of prisoners cannot be tolerated by a civilized society, this seems to make the seizure unreasonable even
by the Court's own lights. If we were now to argue that legitimate institutional goals outweigh Palmer's interests, this would not be a strong argument: "Depriving inmates of any residuum of privacy or possessory rights is
in fact plainly *contrary* to institutional goals. Sociologists recognize that prisoners deprived of any sense of individuality devalue themselves and others
and therefore are more prone to violence toward themselves or others"
(420). Although Stevens cites a number of recent studies that support this
conclusion, in the final analysis, the argument that institutional needs outweigh Palmer's rights needs no such sociological evidence to rebut it. It is

sufficiently rebutted by the fact that prison rules themselves permitted Palmer to possess this property. There can be no institutional need for sei- zure and destruction of items that are defined by the rules themselves as non-contraband: "To accord prisoners any less protection is to declare that the prisoners are entitled to no measure of human dignity or individuality— not a photo, a letter, nor anything except standard-issue prison clothing would be free from arbitrary seizure and destruction. Yet that is the view the Court takes today. It declares prisoners to be little more than chattels, a view I thought society had outgrown long ago" (420).

Stevens ends with a more general set of reflections. Citing a 1974 case in which it was firmly asserted that prisoners are not wholly stripped of consti- tutional protections, he insists that traditionally the courts have a special duty to protect the rights of the powerless and the outcast against claims of mere expediency:

> The courts, of course, have a special obligation to protect the rights of pris- oners. Prisoners are truly the outcasts of society. Disenfranchised, scorned and feared, often deservedly so, shut away from public view, prisoners are surely a "discrete and insular minority." In this case, the destruction of Palmer's property was a seizure; the Judiciary has a constitutional duty to determine whether it was justified. . . .
>
> By telling prisoners that no aspect of their individuality, from a photo of a child to a letter from a wife, is entitled to constitutional protection, the Court breaks with the ethical tradition that I had thought was enshrined forever in our jurisprudence. (420)

My concern, in assessing this opinion, is not centrally with the merits of its constitutional argument. What, then, is the relevance of what might be called the literary aspects of Stevens's consideration of Palmer? First we must describe these aspects. Stevens's opinion is not especially emotional in any obvious sense. Nor is it rhetorically and stylistically self-conscious; it is not "literary" in the sense of being stylistically impressive. It does, however, seem to me to embody some of the most important traits of the literary "judicious spectator" whom I have imagined. Consider the view of Palmer with which the opinion presents us. Like Louisa Gradgrind face to face with the individuality of one of the Coketown "Hands," Stevens confronts the separateness and individuality of Palmer the prisoner, imagining the signifi- cance of trivial items such as letters and photos for his humanity and his hope of a better life. Rather than treating the prisoner simply as a body to be managed by institutional rules, he treats him as a citizen with rights and with a dignity that calls forth respect. He is able to enter into the existence of one who is (rightly) feared and loathed by society, seeing the interests and rights of the prisoner, and his special circumstances, without fully sharing his emotions and motives. Whereas the majority opinion showed no concern to imagine the prisoner's legitimate interest in his property, Stevens does imagine this interest, in a way that both takes cognizance of the difference between the prisoner and other citizens and, at the same time, recognizes the common human concerns that connect them—concerns for family, for reminders of home, for self-improvement. Stevens positions himself as a neutral and impartial spectator; he is careful to indicate that his reasoning is not ad hoc or tailored to an immediate political result. Indeed, he generalizes about the class of prisoners throughout, emphasizing the representative character of the case and thus the universalizable character of his judgment. In that way his opinion is closely linked, in literary terms, to the generalizing strategies of the ancient tragic chorus: one might compare Sophocles' depiction of the outcast Philoctetes, with his small sunless cave, his rudimentary cup, the disfiguring wound that revolted all normal citizens.

How are these "literary" aspects of the opinion relevant to the case? The majority claimed that institutional expediency took precedence over the prisoner's claims; in so arguing, they obscured from view the humanity of the prisoner, the interests and rights that link him to other constitutionally protected members of society. Stevens's depiction of those common interests gives vivid support to his contention that Palmer has legitimate possessory interests, that these have been invaded, and that the search is in that sense "unreasonable." He might have made the same argument without these vivid details, but they remind us forcefully of the general point that prisoners are citizens and do have rights, that they may not be treated as mere means. It is noteworthy that the majority opinion concurs in these general sentiments, insisting that a civilized society will not tolerate merely malicious searches. Stevens's imagining of the case gives those ideas a life that they lacked in the reflections of the majority and thus makes clear the depth of the problem of consistency in their opinion.

At the same time, the literary aspects of the opinion bear on the question of Hudson's malice. If we can imagine the items seized in the shakedown search—a photograph, a letter—and imagine not only the fact that Palmer possessed these items legitimately but also the character of the interest he was likely to have in these fragile signs of his humanity, we are likely to appreciate more intensely the malicious nature of the intrusion of the guard, whose destruction of a photograph served no conceivable institutional goal other than intimidation and humiliation. The majority have said that intentional harassment and maliciously motivated searches "cannot be tolerated in a civilized society." By imagining the case precisely, Stevens is able to make a strong argument that this case is of exactly that sort. In short, Stevens could have made his argument without the elements I have called "literary." But these elements contribute to his argument that the search was unreasonable and that it constituted malicious intentional harassment of the sort that the majority had judged intolerable.

Stevens's concluding general reflection grows out of, and is buttressed by, his way of imagining the prisoner's dignity and humanity. He reflects that in general the Constitution stands between human beings and unfettered expediency, that the liberty interests protected in the Fourth Amendment are valued so highly that they are protected against expediency arguments as a matter of constitutional principle. This is no truism. It is an understanding of constitutional reasoning fundamentally at odds, for example, with Posner's economic approach, according to which these liberty interests would in fact become a matter of expediency.[17] Posner himself has more recently granted that liberty interests protected in the Constitution cannot be fully explained on his economic model.[18] Stevens makes a case for the more traditional way of viewing liberty interests; the case derives support from his ability to see and describe the value of the liberty interests at issue and their connection with human individuality.

Mary J. Carr v. Allison Gas Turbine Division, General Motors Corporation, U.S. Court of Appeals for the Seventh Circuit, July 26, 1994.
[Opinion by Richard Posner.]

Mary Carr was the first woman to work in the tinsmith shop of the gas turbine division of General Motors at their plant in Indiana. Over a period of five years, she encountered sexual harassment from her male coworkers. During four of the five years she complained to her supervisor, to no avail. In 1989 she decided that the situation had become unbearable and quit. She brought suit against General Motors, seeking back pay and other relief. After a bench trial, District Judge Larry J. McKinney ruled in favor of GM, accepting GM's argument that the alleged harassment was merely sexual bantering of a type common in the workplace, and that GM was powerless to stop this bantering. On appeal, the court ruled in favor of Mary Carr.[19]

The case is relatively unusual in that the court overruled the district judge on the findings of fact. At the opening of the opinion, Posner remarks that Carr's lawyers, concerned that the required "clear-error" standard would make such a result unlikely, attempted to persuade the court that there had been legal error in the district court opinion. Posner found no legal error, but he did find error in the findings of fact. The "clear-error" standard "requires us appellate judges to distinguish between the situation in which we *think* that if we had been the trier of fact we would have decided the case differently and the situation in which we are *firmly convinced* that we would have done so." Posner thus announces at the start (referring to a usual standard) that his ruling is based on this sort of firm conviction. His account of the facts must now support that judgment.

When we speak of "facts" in this case, we must be aware that these are not "facts" as distinct from values and evaluation. There is no dispute about the incidents that occurred in the tinsmith's shop. What is in dispute is their human meaning—how intimidating they were, how adversely they affected the climate in which Carr worked. The relevant facts, then, are human facts of the sort the literary judge is well equipped to ascertain. The questions before Posner, he says, were two: "whether the plaintiff was, because of her sex, subjected to such hostile, intimidating, or degrading behavior, verbal or nonverbal, as to affect adversely the conditions under which she worked"; and "whether, if so, the defendant's reponse or lack thereof to its employees' behavior was negligent" (1009). (A third question raised by the district judge, "whether it was unwelcome harassment," is dismissed by Posner as a nonquestion: "'Welcome sexual harassment' is an oxymoron" [1008]) We may expect that to resolve such questions of "fact" will require a good deal of "fancy." We should note that the relevance of these questions is dictated by Title VII, and not by Posner's untethered imagining. If there had been no law authorizing him to look for human facts of this nature, he would have had no basis for everything that follows. On the other hand, Title VII, as written, clearly needs supplementation from the judge, who must ascertain human facts of this type.

Having given his view on the technical issue of "firm conviction," and having articulated the questions to be asked about the facts, Posner now tells Mary Carr's story:

Carr was a drill operator in GM's gas turbine division when, in August 1984, she entered the skilled trades in the division as a tinsmith apprentice. She was the first woman to work in the tinsmith shop, and her male coworkers were unhappy about working with a woman. They made derogatory comments of a sexual character to her on a daily basis (such as, "I won't work with any cunt"), continually referred to her in her presence by such terms as "whore," "cunt," and "split tail," painted "cunt" on her toolbox, and played various sex- or gender-related pranks on her, such as painting her tool box pink and (without her knowledge) cutting out the seat of her overalls. They festooned her tool box and work area with signs, pictures, and graffitti of an offensive sexual character, hid and stole her tools, hid her toolbox, hung nude pin-ups around the shop, and would strip to their underwear in front of her when changing into and out of their work clothes. One of them placed an obscene Valentine Day's card, addressed to "Cunt," on her toolbox. The card shows a man carrying a naked woman upside down, and the text explains that the man has finally discovered why a woman has two holes—so that she can be carried like a six-pack. A worker named Beckham twice exhibited his penis. The first time, during an argument in which Carr told him the exit door "swings both ways," meaning that he could leave as easily as she could, he replied that he had something that "swings," and he demonstrated. The second time, another male worker bet Beckham $5 that he would not expose himself. He lost the bet, although it is unclear whether Carr was in front of Beckham or behind him. And it was Beckham who told Carr on another occasion that if he fell from a dangerous height in the shop she would have to give him "mouth to dick" resuscitation. Carr's male coworkers urinated from the roof of the shop in her presence, and, in her hearing, one of them accused a black employee who was only intermittently hostile to Carr of being "after that white pussy, that is why you want a woman here, you want some of that." A number of racist remarks and practical jokes of a racial nature were directed against this, the only black employee among the tinsmiths. A frequent remark heard around the shop was, "I'll never retire from this tinsmith position

because it would make an opening for a nigger or a woman." Another of
Carr's male coworkers threw a burning cigarette at her. (1009–10)

Carr began complaining to her immediate supervisor, Jim Routh,

> to no avail. He testified that even though some of the offensive statements
> were made in his presence, not being a woman himself he was not sure that
> the statements would be considered offensive by a woman. His perplexity
> was such that when he heard the statements he would just chuckle and bite
> down harder on his pipe. (1010)

This description is in one sense straightforward; but it manifests considerable literary selectivity and skill. Posner positions himself close to the
scene—he narrates the facts in more detail than is strictly necessary. And
yet his stance is that of a judicious observer whose attitude to the conduct
of the male workers is highly critical. The sardonic use of words such as
"festooned" and "the text explains," his insistence on the both offensive and
threatening character of the workers' behavior to Carr, and especially his
vivid satirical portrait of Routh ("his perplexity was such") tell us that he sees
through the argument (made by GM throughout) that all this was merely a
kind of joking or prank-playing in which workers of both sexes engaged. He
positions himself as someone who (unlike Routh) can imagine the likely impact of this conduct on a female employee.

Posner now confronts the question of impact directly, addressing himself
to the district judge's contention that the tinsmiths' behavior was not harassing, since offensive language is common in the workplace, and employers
are not under a legal obligation to purify the workplace of this language just
because some people find it offensive. We must, Posner argues, insist on the
difference between the "merely vulgar and mildly offensive" and the
"deeply offensive and sexually harassing." He attempts to articulate that distinction by considering Carr's situation:

> For one thing, the words and acts of which she complains were, unlike what
> may have been the situation in [another relevant case] targeted on her, and
> it is a lot more uncomfortable to be the target of offensive words and con-
> duct than to be merely an observer of them. Patricia J. Williams, *The Alchemy
> of Race and Rights: Diary of a Law Professor* 129 (1991). For another thing, defac-
> ing a person's property (even if it is hers just to use while at work) and muti-

lating her clothing (even if it is hers just to wear while at work) are more
ominous, more aggressive affronts than mere words. (1010)

Here we see a use of empathy in connection with judicious assessment. It
is interesting that Posner, who is well known for using many fewer citations
and footnotes than most judges, and who is personally responsible for the
citations in his opinions,[20] cites the work of legal scholar Patricia Williams
on race as a source for his conclusions in this paragraph. He seems to be
suggesting that his complete assessment of Carr's contention requires comparison with other narratives from people in relevantly similar positions of
social inequality. (The connection between sexual and racial harassment
had already been made in the description of the tinsmiths' treatment of the
black coworker who refused to join fully in their anti-Carr campaign.) It was
perhaps not easy for a judge in Posner's position to decide, on the basis of
his own judgment and experience, whether the intimidation reported by
Carr was reasonably based in the objective facts of her situation. Part of his
solution was to consider other stories of harassment. Viewed as a deliberately chosen literary device, the Williams reference demonstrates a determination to try to get close to the experience of people in positions of inequality, as if that is a factor relevant to the correct resolution of the legal question
of fact.

Posner now turns to the district judge's contention that the behavior,
though harassing, was not unwelcome to Carr, who herself used words like
"fuck head" and "dick head," who once placed her hand on the thigh of a
male coworker, and, who, "when shown a pornographic picture and asked
to point out the clitoris, obliged." She provoked misconduct, in short, because she was "unladylike," to use the district judge's word. Posner comments:

> Even if we ignore the question why "unladylike" behavior should provoke
> not a vulgar response but a hostile, harassing response, and even if Carr's
> testimony that she talked and acted as she did in an effort to be "one of the
> boys" is (despite its plausibility) discounted, her words and conduct cannot
> be compared to those of the men and used to justify their conduct and
> exonerate their employer. . . . The asymmetry of positions must be consid-
> ered. She was one woman; they were many men. Her use of terms like
> "fuck head" could not be deeply threatening, or her placing a hand on
> the thigh of one of her macho coworkers intimidating; and it was not she

who brought the pornographic picture to the "anatomy lesson." We have trouble *imagining* a situation in which male factory workers sexually harass a lone woman *in self-defense* as it were; yet that at root is General Motors' characterization of what happened here. (1011)

This is a calm and entirely unsentimental paragraph. Posner is not wringing his hands or emoting in the manner of one personally caught up in the situation. In all respects, he is the judicious spectator. But he does seem to fulfill Smith's conception of that quasi-literary role. His test is, in effect, one of "fancy": try to imagine the situation as the male workers describe it, in which Carr was just as threatening to them as they to her, and you find you can't do it. (Note the italicization of *imagine*.) But picture the asymmetry of the situation as it was, picture Carr's isolation and her lack of support from the supervisor, and you come to the conclusion that she was the victim of a campaign of harassment of remarkable duration and intensity. (Discussing Carr's difficult personal situation in the following paragraph—her foster son was executed for murder—Posner takes the opportunity to mention that "one of the charming comments that Beckham, the coworker who had exposed himself to her, had made to her was that he would have been happy to pay the electrical bill for the execution.")

Did GM act improperly? Posner argues that negligence was proved, despite the fact that GM claims to have been the victim of "a conspiracy of silence among the tinsmiths"—a phrase that leaves the reader in no doubt of Posner's critical response. He concludes, "We do not find the picture of mighty GM helpless in the face of the foul-mouthed tinsmiths remotely plausible." Here, once again, appeal to the imagination yields the judicious spectator's sardonic response. Posner then comments, with respect to Carr's situation, that to obtain "remedy for constructive discharge" she need show simply "that the discrimination to which she was subjected was sufficiently serious to cause a reasonable person to quit"—a standard that in effect incorporates the responses of the judicious spectator into the resolution of the case.

We now arrive at Posner's conclusion:

It is difficult for an employer to sort out charges and countercharges of sexual harassment among feuding employees, but we are dealing here with a situation in which for years one of the nation's largest enterprises found

itself helpless to respond effectively to an egregious campaign of sexual harassment directed at one woman. No reasonable person could imagine that
General Motors was genuinely helpless, that it did all it reasonably could
have done. The evidence is plain that it (or at least its gas turbine division)
was unprepared to deal with problems of sexual harassment even when
those problems were rubbed in its face, and also incapable of improvising
a solution. Its efforts at investigation were lackluster, its disciplinary efforts
nonexistent, its remedial efforts perfunctory. The U.S. Navy has been able
to integrate women into the crews of warships; General Motors should have
been able to integrate one woman into a tinsmith shop.

   The judgment is reversed with instructions to enter judgment on liability
for the plaintiff (since no other result would be consistent with the record . . .) and proceed to a determination of the remedy to which she is entitled. (1012–13)

Posner concludes with a direct appeal to the imaginings and responses of
a "reasonable person"—a traditional common-law standard closely linked
to Smith's judicious-spectator norm. He shows in his prose the well-founded
indignation and contempt such a spectator feels at the behavior of GM. In
literary terms, the paragraph seems to make reference to the traditional de-
vices and emotions of the genre of satire, whether in its ancient Roman form
(Juvenal) or in more recent exemplars such as the works of Swift. (The *saeva
indignatio* mentioned in Swift's epitaph is, perhaps, the emotion Posner's
prose is attempting to construct.) He denounces the pretense that GM was
helpless and expresses his view of both GM and the tinsmiths in the metaphorical "even when those problems were rubbed in its face"—comparing
GM to an incontinent dog who has to have its nose rubbed in its own
shit. The rhetorically effective sentence beginning "Its efforts" expresses
indignation in a tricolon of ascending condemnation; the following sentence uses the parallel "been able to integrate" to bring home the disparity between the task faced (and accomplished) by the Navy and the task
refused by GM.

   Posner carefully positions himself as a judge and a spectator, detached
and neutral in the appropriate ways. But imagination and appropriate emotion are crucial in the reasoning of his opinion. His indignation is not capricious: it is solidly grounded in the facts, and he can make his reader feel it
in his narration of the facts. Indeed, his opinion does what good satire of the

Juvenalian or Swiftean kind does: it inspires indignation through the mordant portrayal of human venality and cruelty. Here as in the Stevens opinion, the literary approach is closely connected with sympathetic attention to the special plight of people who are socially unequal and to a certain extent, therefore, helpless. Posner repeatedly draws attention to this aspect of his thinking, and to its relevance in answering the legal questions about intimidation and hostility. As Posner writes: "The asymmetry of positions must be considered."

Bowers v. Hardwick, U.S. Supreme Court, 1986.
[Opinions by Justices White and Burger.]

Both the case and the opinions are famous; I shall therefore do less summarizing than in the other cases.[21] But let us set the stage briefly. Michael Hardwick was in a bedroom in his apartment engaged in fellatio with another man, when he was arrested by a police officer who had entered the apartment to serve an arrest warrant on Hardwick for drinking in public. Both men were arrested for violating the state's sodomy law, held in jail, and released without charges being lodged against them. Hardwick brought a suit to invalidate the law. The law itself was worded in terms of sexual acts, defining sodomy as either oral or anal intercourse. As is frequently the case in sodomy statutes, the offense was not restricted to homosexuals, and a heterosexual couple, "John and Mary Doe," later joined the suit, though their case never reached the Supreme Court. The district court held that they "had neither sustained, nor were in any immediate danger of sustaining, any direct injury from the enforcement of the statute." The Court of Appeals affirmed the district court's judgment, dismissing the Does' claim for lack of standing.[22] In this way the record virtually acknowledged that the statute would not be enforced against heterosexuals.

The majority and concurring opinions in *Bowers* have been criticized often, and from many different points of view. In assessing the literary or nonliterary aspects of the opinions, we must first of all consider the case as a due process case, as it was actually argued. It will then be relevant to ask how aspects of the literary imagination would prove relevant to arguing this or a similar case as an equal protection case (a line of argument suggested in Justice Blackmun's dissent, and in recent legal scholarship on the topic).

The question before the Court, since the case was argued as a due process case, was whether the alleged right to consensual homosexual sodomy was in fact a privacy right entailed by previous Fourteenth Amendment privacy cases. The Court notes that the category of rights in question has been identified as including "those fundamental liberties that are 'implicit in the concept of ordered liberty' [and those that are] 'deeply rooted in this Nation's history and tradition.'" It is important to note these constraints on the result and the reasoning of the case. Any sympathy or imagination exercised by any of the opinions will be irrelevant unless it either illuminates the connection between this case and relevant precedents or helps us decide whether the case fits one or both of the two general descriptions deriving from earlier cases.

Concerning the precedents, Justice White reviews the privacy cases and finds

> that none of the rights announced in those cases bears any resemblance to the claimed constitutional right of homosexuals to engage in acts of sodomy that is asserted in this case. No connection between family, marriage, or procreation on the one hand and homosexual activity on the other has been demonstrated. . . . Moreover, any claim that these cases nevertheless stand for the proposition that any kind of private sexual conduct between consenting adults is constitutionally insulated from state proscription is unsupportable. (190–91)

This certainly offers a plausible reading of the privacy cases. It is indeed true that *Griswold* focuses on decisional privacy in the context of the marital relationship with reference to decisions about childbearing. Although *Eisenstadt* extends this right to unmarried individuals, and thus recognizes a decisional privacy right of individuals rather than couples, it still focuses on decisions involving whether or not to bear a child. The same is the case in *Roe v. Wade*. The majority in *Eisenstadt* hold that "[i]f the right of privacy means anything, it is the right of the *individual*, married or single, to be free from unwarranted governmental intrusion into matters so fundamentally affecting a person as the decision whether to bear or beget a child." This wording suggests that there might be other fundamental person-affecting rights in this area. But no other rights are named; and since *Eisenstadt* was tried as an equal protection case, its central line of argument was simply that whatever contraception rights married people have must belong to the unmarried as well. The step from *Eisenstadt* and *Roe* to the acknowledgment of a right of consenting adults to engage in the sexual conduct of their choice is not long, but one must grant that this step had not previously been taken.[23]

What could the relevance of literary imagining possibly have been to the determination whether this step should have been taken? What we find in the previous privacy cases is a consideration of the way in which the recognized privacy rights shield liberties of personal choice in intimate matters fundamentally affecting one's personhood. Given the unclarity about the range of this protection, one would expect that a thorough sifting of the question involved in *Bowers* should involve a close consideration of the person-affecting character of the privacy right claimed by Hardwick. The majority opinion maintains a lofty distance from the facts of Michael Hardwick's situation.[24] The distancing language ("the claimed constitutional right of homosexuals to engage in acts of sodomy") expresses a refusal to think about how Hardwick's personhood is affected by the issue, and even seems to express a somewhat sardonic attitude toward his suggestion that the right involved does deserve protection. Indeed, throughout the opinion there seems to be a marked effort to keep the human story at a distance, not to describe the events as if they happened to someone one might know or even be. A more empathetic consideration of the situation of someone whose chosen form of consensual sexual conduct is illegal might not have changed the judgment about how to read the precedents. But it would have promoted a full and thorough consideration of the question of the reach of the privacy right, which does not seem to have taken place here, so rapidly is Hardwick's contention dismissed.

Indeed, we may note that the relationship of this case to fundamental issues of personhood receives far less discussion than took place in a far more trivial case (at least in the dissenting opinion). In *Kelley v. Johnson* the issue concerned a police department regulation limiting the length of policemen's hair.[25] This was occasion for a substantial discussion (by the dissenters) of the relationship of personal appearance to integrity and personal identity, and all of these to the privacy right. Surely Hardwick's case, in addition to its greater human urgency, lay far closer to the precedents and involved a right that could with far more plausibility have been connected to them.

If we turn to the next question, whether the alleged right fits one or both of the two relevant general descriptions, we find again, in both the majority and the concurring opinions, a detached and markedly non-narrative approach: "Proscriptions against that conduct have ancient roots," write the majority, dismissing the idea that a right to commit homosexual sodomy is either "implicit in the concept of ordered liberty" or "deeply rooted in this Nation's history and tradition." Chief Justice Burger's concurring opinion is even more severe. Burger states that "decisions of individuals relating to homosexual conduct have been subject to state intervention throughout the history of Western civilization." He notes that "Blackstone described 'the infamous *crime against nature*' as an offense of 'deeper malignity' than rape, a heinous act 'the very mention of which is a disgrace to human nature,' and 'a crime not fit to be named.' . . . To hold that the act of homosexual sodomy is somehow protected as a fundamental right would be to cast aside millennia of moral teaching." The severity of Burger's language, as well as his lengthy enumeration of such historical condemnations, serves to distance the Court, and the reader, even further from the perspective and story of Michael Hardwick himself, a human being seeking to live a fully human life. We are encouraged to see Hardwick as a dangerous criminal, similar to a rapist, and nothing in the way the facts of his story are related informs us otherwise.

Closely connected to this distancing strategy, I believe, is the fact that we find in the opinions no argument concerning the all-important question of level of generality. Surely it is obvious that, described at a highly specific level as "a right to commit homosexual sodomy," the right in question is not traditional, and that it has not been traditionally considered to be implicit in the concept of ordered liberty. On the other hand, were the right in question understood generally, as a right to determine the course of one's own sexual life, provided that one does not harm others, it could at least be argued that such a right was recognized in a variety of previous cases, for example, those involving the right to marry a partner of one's choice. The dissenters do so argue, connecting sodomy laws to laws forbidding miscegenation. (Miscegenation described concretely—as "marriage to a partner of a different race" rather than "marriage to a partner of one's choice"—was of course not a traditionally recognized fundamental right; described generally, it did involve such a right.) But there is no attempt here to discuss this vital issue, so evident does it seem to the majority that homosexual sex is unrelated to other liberty interests in the area of sex and marriage. This avoidance of argument is facilitated by treating the homosexual like a pariah, whom centuries of history have concurred in condemning. If it seemed to Blackstone disgraceful even to mention such acts, it is easy to justify not dwelling on them very long in thought and argument, in order to work out properly their relationship to other acts.

What would one expect from the literary imagination here, and what relevance might it have? One would expect, I think, two things that were sorely lacking in the majority and concurring opinions: a careful attention to history and social context, and an empathetic consideration of the situation of the homosexual in American society. History first. The historical claims made in the opinions are imprecise and, to a great extent, false. Study of the history of sexual conceptions and practices is a burgeoning area of scholarship in many fields of the humanities and social sciences. Books that are not at all beyond the reach of a nonspecialist have by now exploded the simple picture of a history of condemnation on which the majority rely, in the case of Greco-Roman, Christian, Jewish, and English traditions.[26] The contemporary debate in each of the major religious and philosophical traditions of the world is complicated, and there is no major group in which there is not internal debate and ferment.[27] The literary judge would wish to "read" Michael Hardwick's case in its full historical and social context. This would entail getting the history right, if one appealed to it at all.

Getting the history right might or might not affect the result—for one could still argue that the right level on which to define the relevant rights was the most specific level and that the relevant Anglo-American legal traditions still would not uphold the classification of the right in question, specifically defined, as "implicit in the concept of ordered liberty" or "deeply rooted in this Nation's history and tradition." But understanding how other times and places have viewed similar conduct would have provided a much-needed basis for considering the possible relevance of a more general level of description. This same process would have been very much advanced by considering in an empathetic manner what was actually at stake for Hardwick in the case. Such consideration—of which Forster's *Maurice* gives us one vivid example—would at least have raised, if not settled, the question of the relationship between this right and the traditionally protected rights to marry and to control one's own reproductive choices.

In these ways, the literary element in judging might have contributed to a fuller deliberation about aspects of the case, even as it was actually argued, as a due process case. Had the case been argued as an equal protection case, the relevance of the imagination would have been clearer still. Justice Blackmun in dissent recognizes that the case has a serious equal protection aspect and might have been argued in this way. More recently, Cass Sunstein has argued that the equal protection route would have been preferable in the case, given his view that the due process clause is typically backward-looking and tradition-respecting, the equal protection clause forward-looking and reform-oriented.[28] Since *Bowers* as decided has now blocked the due process route, it is also important to note that similar cases might still be argued by appeal to equal protection. Equal protection argument typically requires consideration of the history of discrimination under which a group has labored, as well as its circumstances of political powerlessness. Consideration of a more detailed, empathetic, and concrete sort would have contributed to revealing a history of discrimination that brings this case into a close relation with other histories of the persecution of marginalized and despised groups.[29] Indeed, it would appear that this sort of inquiry is not only sufficient for that understanding, but necessary as well—for without it, it is difficult to make the all-important distinction between Michael Hardwick's situation and that of a violent criminal (the rapist mentioned by Burger), whose acts are subject to penalty for very good reasons. In order to think well about an equal protection argument, we have to be able to separate irrational discrimination from condemnation of what is genuinely dangerous. An understanding of the history of the prejudice against homosexuals in American society—combined with awareness of different attitudes in other cultures and with a sympathetic understanding of the aims and intentions of actual homosexuals—would, I believe, show that this group is relevantly similar to racial minorities, women, and national minorities, rather than to rapists or to child molesters. It would be difficult to get to this result without using the imagination, while treating homosexuals with the repugnance and distance shown in the majority and concurring opinions.

The constitutional issues bearing on this case are highly complex and are disputed at every point. A judge deciding such a case is constrained in many ways by text, history, and precedent. It would be foolish to claim that the literary imagination does all the work here, and inappropriate to recommend that it work outside these institutional constraints. On the other hand, within these constraints it can supply insights that should prove valuable to a complete deliberation on the relevant issues.

Does literary judging make a difference? Not in all imaginable cases, obviously. Sometimes the legal issues tell clearly one way or another; sometimes the facts are so simple and uncontroversial that literary imagining is not important. In all cases, the law must first of all be there, or no judge can do anything. Justice Stevens's interest in Palmer's photos and letters goes nowhere without the text of the Constitution, a range of specific precedents, and the admission by the majority itself that merely malicious and harassing searches are intolerable. Judge Posner would have been powerless to rule on behalf of Mary Carr without Title VII, however much he abhorred sexual harassment. Legislators, too, and the citizens who elect them, need to exercise imagination. The notorious difficulties surrounding the scope and the very existence of the privacy right show how difficult it is for judges to rule innovatively, even to plug what might seem a gap in the explicit text of the Constitution; and even given that history of judicial intervention, no clear result in Hardwick's case is determined. Empathetic citizens should not rely on the judiciary alone to require what they think just.

But in these three cases—two of which involve highly contested constitutional questions and the third of which involves a deep disagreement about how to assess the facts—the full, precise, and judicious imagining of the human facts did make or would possibly make at least some difference to the result: in *Hudson*, by giving Stevens a sense of the importance for Palmer of the property interest Hudson had maliciously violated; in *Mary Carr*, by giving Posner a vivid sense of the harassment suffered by Carr and of the implausibility of GM's version of the facts; in *Bowers* as actually argued, possibly, by giving the hypothetical literary judge a sense of the fundamental nature of the rights and liberties involved and their relation to other fundamental liberties; in *Bowers* seen as an equal protection case, by giving the judge an understanding of the special disadvantages faced by gay and lesbian people, of the history of sodomy laws as instruments of discrimination, of the general social stigma associated with being the target of such laws.

In none of the cases do I suggest that ordinary legal reasoning, including prominently the consideration of precedent, should be subordinated to untethered sentiment. The judge is not a legislator, and his imagination must conform to tight institutional constraints. In the *Carr* and *Hudson* opinions, the sentiments of sympathy and indignation that are expressed are valuable precisely because they are connected to good legal reasoning of a traditional sort and to a solid grasp of the facts. But in both cases we can say, I think, that the literary judge has a better grasp of the totality of the facts than the nonliterary judge. My claim is, then, that literary judging is by no means sufficient for good judging, and could certainly be pernicious if not properly tethered to other purely institutional and legal virtues; but we should demand it in appropriate circumstances, whatever else we also demand.

Attesting Sympathy

I now return to Whitman, for I have come round to several themes that lie at the heart of his poetry: the pain of social exclusion; the relationship between the exclusion of the homosexual and other exclusions based on gender and religion and race; the interest all citizens have in liberty, erotic and otherwise; the importance of fostering a political rationality that can "see into" that interest, with what Whitman calls the poet's "Soul of love and tongue of fire!/ Eye to pierce the deepest deeps and sweep the world!" I have suggested, with Whitman, that a literary imagining of the importance of various liberty and equality interests for citizens offers valuable guidance in cases dealing with those interests. So I shall conclude by discussing a famous section of Whitman's *Song of Myself* in which all these themes are brought together with compression and poignancy. The passage comes about halfway through the poem, after a section in which the poet-speaker houses a runaway slave, tending the sores left by the irons on his legs and ankles, and after the parable "Twenty-eight young men bathe by the shore," a vivid lyrical description of the exclusion of the female from full inclusion and equality as a sexual being. "I am he attesting sympathy," summarizes the poet. He then announces that in and through his imagination the excluded find speech and their emotions find recognition:

> Unscrew the locks from the doors!
> Unscrew the doors themselves from their jambs!

Whoever degrades another degrades me,
And whatever is done or said returns at last to me . . .

I speak the pass-word primeval, I give the sign of democracy,
By God! I will accept nothing which all cannot have their counterpart of
    on the same terms.

Through me many long dumb voices,
Voices of the interminable generations of prisoners and slaves,
Voices of the diseas'd and despairing and of thieves and dwarfs,
Voices of cycles of preparation and accretion,
And of the threads that connect the stars, and of wombs and of the
    father-stuff,
And of the rights of them the others are down upon,
Of the deform'd, trivial, flat, foolish, despised,
Fog in the air, beetles rolling balls of dung,

Through me forbidden voices,
Voices of sexes and lusts, voices veil'd and I remove the veil,
Voices indecent by me clarified and transfigur'd. . . .

Dazzling and tremendous how quick the sun-rise would kill me,
If I could not now and always send sun-rise out of me.

Here Whitman summarizes his account of the poet's democratizing mission. It is a mission of imagination, inclusion, sympathy, and voice. The poet is the instrument through which the "long dumb voices" of the excluded come forth from their veils and into the light. To attend to the way things are with the excluded and the despised as well as the powerful, to insist on participating oneself, through sympathy, in the degradation of the degraded, to accept only what others can have on the same terms, to give voice to the pain of the excluded, the intimidation of the harassed—this is a norm of democratic judgment highly pertinent to the situation of Bigger Thomas, of Forster's Maurice, of Mary Carr, of the prisoner Palmer, of Michael Hardwick. Whitman is especially insistent that the poet's speech will remove the veil from the voices of those silenced by sexual exclusion and opprobrium. He claims that the light of the poetic imagination is a crucial agent of democratic equality for these and other excluded people, since only that imagination will get the facts of their lives right, and see in their unequal treatment a degradation of oneself.

I claim that it would be a good thing to have judges who could see into those lines. The imagination involved in them exemplifies a sort of public rationality we badly need at this time in this country, where increasingly we are refusing one another this sort of inclusive vision, closing the doors of sympathy that Whitman wished here to open. The sympathy of the judicious spectator does not by itself dictate any specific result in any particular legal case. It is constrained in many ways by statute and precedent. Nor, even as imagination, does it stand alone: it needs to be able to rely on imagination and compassion already exercised in the legislative sphere. But it does exemplify a type of thinking that should be involved in judicial reflection.

Standing by Blue Ontario's shore, Whitman moves on from his general call for the poet-judge and interrogates prospective candidates for that role. To the person who "would assume a place to teach or be a poet here in the States," he poses a remarkable series of questions:

> Who are you indeed who would talk or sing to America?
> Have you studied out the land, its idioms and men? . . .
> Have you consider'd the organic compact of the first day of the first year
>   of Independence, sign'd by the commissioners, ratified by the States,
>   and read by Washington at the head of the army?
> Have you possess'd yourself of the Federal Constitution?
> Have you sped through fleeting customs, popularities?
> Can you hold your hand against all seductions, follies, whirls, fierce con-
>   tentions? are you very strong? are you really of the whole People?
> Are you not of some coterie? some school or mere religion?
> Do you hold the like love for those hardening to maturity? for the last-
>   born? little and big? and for the errant?

I claim that the standard of judgment constructed in my conception of "poetic justice" passes these tests. Intimate and impartial, loving without bias, thinking of and for the whole rather than as a partisan of some particular group or faction, comprehending in "fancy" the richness and complexity of each citizen's inner world, the literary judge, like Whitman's poet, sees in the blades of grass the equal dignity of all citizens—and more mysterious images, too, of erotic longing and personal liberty. She combines these vi-

sions in judgments that are in many respects different from those recommended by the Gradgrind school. Nor do they achieve abstraction by standing at a lofty remove from the human facts of cases. Nor, finally, are they
skeptical, despairing of good reasons.

As Whitman indicates, "poetic justice" needs a great deal of nonliterary
equipment: technical legal knowledge, a knowledge of history and precedent, a careful attention to proper legal impartiality. The judge must be a
good judge in these respects. But in order to be fully rational, judges must
also be capable of fancy and sympathy. They must educate not only their
technical capacities but also their capacity for humanity. In the absence of
that capacity, their impartiality will be obtuse and their justice blind. In the
absence of that capacity, the "long dumb" voices that seek to speak through
their justice will remain silent, and the "sun-rise" of democratic judgment
will be to that extent veiled. In the absence of that capacity, the "interminable generations of prisoners and slaves" will dwell in pain around us and
have less hope of freedom.

[Notes]

Preface

1. In contrast, in many European countries, philosophy has been centrally involved in public life for far longer.
2. *Woodson v. North Carolina*, 428 U.S. 280, 304 (1976).
3. The course was invented by James Boyd White in the early 1970s, and revived by Richard Posner in the late 1980s.
4. Martha Nussbaum and Amartya Sen, eds., *The Quality of Life* (Oxford: Clarendon Press, 1993), introduction. For the next volume in this series, see Martha Nussbaum and Jonathan Glover, eds., *Women, Culture, and Development* (Oxford: Clarendon Press, 1995), in which Martha Chen's beautifully written field study of women's lives in rural India and Bangladesh makes a narrative contribution of the sort we favor.
5. For versions of Kantian ethics that stress the flexible and virtue-based aspects of Kant's theory, see Barbara Herman, *The Practice of Moral Judgment* (Cambridge: Harvard University Press, 1993); Onora O'Neill, *Construction of Reason* (Cambridge: Cambridge University Press, 1989).
6. Student 1180, as I discovered when the veil of ignorance was removed, is Sophie Clark, a witty tough-minded Englishwoman who has spent some years as the manager of a race track and is now in a joint J.D./Ph.D. program in law and political science.
7. Henry James, Art of the Novel (New York, 1907) 223–24.
8. Oliver Wendell Holmes, Jr., Letter to Lewis Einstein, July 23, 1906, in *The Essential Holmes,* ed. Richard Posner (Cambridge: Harvard University Press, 1991).

1. The Literary Imagination

1. Charles Dickens, *Hard Times*, ed. David Craig (Harmondsworth: Penguin, 1969), 63 (all citations are from this edition). The studies of the novel from which I have learned most are Raymond Williams, *Culture and Society, 1780–1950* (London: Penguin, 1958), part 1, chap. 5; Craig's excellent introduction to the Penguin edition; and F. R. Leavis, *The Great Tradition* (New York: Charles Scribner's Sons, 1948).

2. As will become plain, I am focusing only on certain sorts of novels here, and I am interested both in features that could be said to be features of the genre and in features specific to the particular author and work.

3. See also a related discussion of these questions in my *Love's Knowledge: Essays on Philosophy and Literature* (New York: Oxford University Press, 1990).

4. Aristotle, *Poetics* 9.

5. See Lucretius, *On the Nature of the Universe*, trans. R. E. Latham and J. Godwin (London: Penguin, 1994), book 1, ll. 926–50.

6. See my discussion in *Upheavals of Thought: A Theory of the Emotions*, the Gifford Lectures for 1993 (Cambridge: Cambridge University Press, forthcoming 1997).

7. See, for example, Stanley Cavell, *Pursuits of Happiness: The Hollywood Comedy of Remarriage* (Cambridge: Harvard University Press, 1981).

8. One might ask about modern drama, but I believe that it would be sanguine to suppose that this is on the whole a living genre, given the constraints exacted by commercialization in the New York theater. Commercialization need not have a stifling effect on quality, but this seems on the whole to have happened in this case. There are individual artists who continue to produce wonderful work, of course; and it would be valuable to compare that work to the novel, although I shall not do so here.

9. Wayne C. Booth, *The Company We Keep: An Ethics of Fiction* (Berkeley and Los Angeles: University of California Press, 1988), 70–77. Booth is not talking only about novels, but his analysis applies above all to the reading of fictional genres.

10. I do not include modern realist versions of tragedy, which are heavily influenced, I believe, by the success of the novel and share many of its features.

11. See Ian Watt, *The Rise of the Novel* (Berkeley and Los Angeles: University of California Press, 1957), and Charles Taylor, *Sources of the Self: The Making of Modern Identity* (Cambridge: Harvard University Press, 1989).

12. See Booth, *The Company We Keep*, chaps. 6–7, esp. 201–5.

13. This way of putting the project has obvious links to John Rawls's portrayal of the search for "reflective equilibrium" in *A Theory of Justice* (Cambridge: Harvard University Press, 1971).

2. Fancy

1. This distinction is very well captured in Henry Richardson, *Practical Reasoning about Final Ends* (Cambridge: Cambridge University Press, 1994), whose account of the commensurability project, and its flaws, is among the very best available (chaps. 5 and 6). For other valuable criticisms of economic utilitarianism, see Amartya Sen and Bernard Williams, introduction to *Utilitarianism and Beyond* (Cambridge: Cambridge University Press, 1988); see also many writings of Sen, including "Plural Utility" in *Choice, Welfare, and Measurement* (Oxford: Basil Blackwell, 1982); *Commodities and Capabilities* (North-Holland, 1985), *The Standard of Living* (Cambridge: Cambridge University Press, 1987).

2. See John Rawls, *A Theory of Justice* (Cambridge: Harvard University Press, 1971), 554–60.

3. Compare the related account in Sen and Williams's introduction to *Utilitarianism and Beyond*, which defines utilitarianism in terms of "welfarism" (information about individual utilities is the only thing about persons that is relevant from the point of view of the theory), "consequentialism" (actions are to be chosen on the basis of the consequences they promote), and "sum-ranking" (the social utility is computed by adding up the individual utilities).

4. Ibid., 4.

5. For a trenchant documentation and critique of these behavioral assumptions, see Amartya Sen, "Rational Fools," *Philosophy and Public Affairs* 6 (1976–77): 317–44, on which more below. Gary Becker's theory of the family (*A Treatise on the Family* [Cambridge: Harvard University Press, 1981]) does posit that the head of the household is an altruist, making arrangements for the well-being of the other family members, but it appears that this is the sense of altruism standard in economics, in which it is construed as a means to promote one's own well-being. There is another and even more salient difficulty with Becker's assumption: it appears (even in this restricted sense of altruism) to be empirically false, at least in many cases in many parts of the world. There are often conflicts for resources within the household, and the head of the household is not always concerned with the well-being of spouse and (especially female) children. See *Women, Culture, and Development*, ed. Martha Nussbaum and Jonathan Glover (Oxford: Clarendon Press, 1995), especially the paper by Sen; also Sen, "Gender and Cooperative Conflicts," in *Persistent Inequalities*, ed. Irene Tinker (New York: Oxford University Press, 1990).

6. For example, it is argued that we do not want doctors who are trying in all their choices to maximize the total of human happiness, asking in each case whether it is better for all humanity that this person lives or dies; the utilitarian result itself may be better promoted by a less calculating and more duty-driven kind

of agent. On all this, see R. M. Hare, *Moral Thinking* (Oxford: Clarendon Press, 1981).

7. See, for example, the criticisms of the Supreme Court's privacy jurisprudence in Richard Posner's *The Economics of Justice* (Cambridge: Harvard University Press, 1981), part 3. In Posner's 1983 preface, he writes: "The book uses economics in two quite different ways, the positive and the normative—and I recognize that the latter is much more controversial. . . . I hope I have not 'oversold' this approach by insufficient attention to the rather bizarre results that its unflinching application could produce." He concludes that we should read him as offering "a subject for speculation" rather than "a blueprint for social action" (v–vi). Other examples of the normative use of wealth-maximization include Tomas J. Philipson and Richard Posner, *Private Choices and Public Health: The AIDS Epidemic in an Economic Perspective* (Cambridge: Harvard University Press, 1993); and Richard Epstein, *Forbidden Grounds* (Cambridge: Harvard University Press, 1993).

8. A recent study has shown that students exposed to this model in economics courses actually become more focused on self-interest and less given to altruism than they were before: see Robert Frank, Thomas Gilovich, and Dennis Regan, "Does Studying Economics Inhibit Cooperation?" *Journal of Economic Perspectives* (Spring 1993), and discussion of the study in "How do you Mean, "Fair"? Economics Focus column in the *Economist,* May 29, 1993.

9. Joel Waldfogel, "The Deadweight Loss of Christmas," *American Economic Review* 83 (1993).

10. Richard Posner, *Sex and Reason* (Cambridge: Harvard University Press, 1992), 119–20.

11. For example, see James Griffin, *Well-Being* (Oxford: Clarendon Press, 1986), and Richard B. Brandt, *A Theory of the Good and Right* (Oxford: Clarendon Press, 1979).

12. See Becker, *A Treatise on the Family,* and Posner, *Sex and Reason.*

13. See Barbara Herrnstein Smith, *Contingencies of Value,* (Cambridge: Harvard University Press, 1988). See also all the writings of Richard Posner, including *Economic Analysis of Law* (Boston: Little, Brown, 1977), *The Economics of Justice,* and *Law and Literature: A Misunderstood Relation* (Cambridge: Harvard University Press, 1988). In *Problems of Jurisprudence* (Cambridge: Harvard University Press, 1990) Posner has modified his approach, espousing a kind of "pragmatism." For a good general critique of economic reasoning in public life, see Sen and Williams's introduction to *Utilitarianism and Beyond.*

14. See Posner, *Economic Analysis of Law* and *The Economics of Justice;* Gary Becker, *The Economic Approach to Human Behavior* (Chicago: University of Chicago Press, 1976), and *A Treatise on the Family.* Especially instructive is the opening of Posner's *The Economics of Justice,* where he first introduces the "assumption that people are rational maximizers of their satisfactions," noting that "the principles of eco-

nomics are deductions from this assumption"—and then goes on to use the word "rational," without further philosophical argument, as if it just *meant* "maximizing satisfactions" (1–2). One trenchant critique of Posner, with regard to the worth of one's personal integrity, is Margaret Jane Radin, "Market-Inalienability," *Harvard Law Review* 100 (1987): 1849 ff. Other valuable critiques of Posner are James Boyd White, "What Can a Lawyer Learn from Literature" (review of Posner's *Law and Literature*) *Harvard Law Review* 102 (1989): 2014–47, and "Economics and Law: Two Cultures in Tension," *Tennessee Law Review* 54 (1986): 161–202; Frank Michelman, "Norms and Normativity in the Economic Theory of Law," *Minnesota Law Review* 62 (1978): 1015 ff.; Arthur Leff, "Economic Analysis of Law: Some Realism about Nominalism," *Virginia Law Review* 60 (1974): 451 ff. For a critique of Posner using literature, see Robin West, "Authority, Autonomy, and Choice: The Role of Consent in the Moral and Political Visions of Franz Kafka and Richard Posner," *Harvard Law Review* 99 (1985): 384 ff. Posner replies in "The Ethical Significance of Free Choice: A Reply to Professor West," *Harvard Law Review* 99 (1986): 1431 ff., and West responds in "Submission, Choice, and Ethics: A Rejoinder to Judge Posner, ibid., 1449 ff. See also Posner, *Law and Literature,* chap. 4, for a later version of his argument.

15. Frank Easterbrook, "Method, Result, and Authority: A Reply," *Harvard Law Review* 98 (1985): 622 ff.; George Stigler, Convocation Address, *University of Chicago Record,* June 1, 1981, 2 (for this reference I am indebted to James White, "Economics and Law," 172).

16. Some of these criticisms do apply, as well, to philosophical utilitarians, many of whom do treat values as commensurable by a single quantitative standard. See, for example, James Griffin, "Are There Incommensurable Values?" *Philosophy and Public Affairs* 7 (1977): 34–59, which I criticize in "The Discernment of Perception," in *Love's Knowledge: Essays on Philosophy and Literature* (New York: Oxford University Press, 1990).

17. For a wonderful account of these contrasts in the opening scene, see F. R. Leavis, *The Great Tradition* (New York: New York University Press, 1948), 227 ff.

18. The students are numbered, not, I add, for the reasons of fairness in grading that motivated the numerical identification that figured in my preface: M'Choakumchild sees which child is which very well indeed and plays favorites constantly.

19. Shortly after this, hearing of Stephen's misfortunes, Louisa remarks that she had previously heard them mentioned, "though I was not attending to the particulars at the time."

20. Contrast, for example, the treatment of choice in John Rawls's Kantian theory, in which satisfactions without choice are counted as having no moral worth (*A Theory of Justice,* section on perfectionism).

21. That this theory is not merely a fiction can be confirmed by reading Becker's *A Treatise on the Family*.

22. Contrast the passage where Louisa sees that her marriage has failed: Because of "all those causes of disparity which arise out of two individual natures, and which no general laws shall ever rule or state for me, father, until they shall be able to direct the anatomist where to strike his knife into the secrets of my soul."

23. This lies very deep in the motivation behind utilitarianism in general, and inspires some of its deliberate departures from ordinary belief. Henry Sidgwick, for example, conceding that to adopt a single metric of choice is to depart from ordinary belief, writes, "If we are not to systematize human activities by taking Universal Happiness as their common end, on what other principles are we to systematize them?"—and remarks that such departures are always found when a science is born (*Methods of Ethics*, 7th ed. [London, 1907], 401, 406, 425).

24. Just before we hear of the "leaden books," the narrator himself describes the people of Coketown as "walking against time towards the infinite world."

25. See Amartya Sen, "Rational Fools."

26. The noncalculative aspects of human behavior, and the frequent irrationality of preferences and desires, have been rigorously analyzed by Jon Elster in *Ulysses and the Sirens* (Cambridge: Cambridge University Press, 1979), and *Sour Grapes: Studies in the Subversion of Rationality* (Cambridge: Cambridge University Press, 1983); there is by now an extensive literature on related matters. As Sen shows, the existence of economic analyses of commitment and sympathy does not necessarily remove the objection, for in accommodating these features of human life to that model, the analysis often subtly but crucially alters them, making them instrumental to the maximization of utility.

27. See especially Jon Elster's *Sour Grapes*, and see also his article "Sour Grapes—Utilitarianism and the Genesis of Wants," in Sen and Williams, *Utilitarianism and Beyond*, 219–38. See the related criticism of deformed preferences in John Harsanyi, "Morality and the Theory of Rational Behaviour," in ibid., 39–62. Related ideas have played a role in Sen's criticism of development economics: see *Resources, Values, and Development* (Oxford: Blackwell, 1984). An analysis of the social formation of emotion and desire is offered in my "Constructing Love, Desire, and Care," forthcoming in *Laws and Nature: Shaping Sex, Preference, and Family*, ed. David Estlund and Martha Nussbaum, (New York: Oxford University Press, 1996).

28. At the same time, the utilitarian's particular conception of science owes something to the Cartesian conception of nature as a machine; this shows up especially clearly in the attitudes to animals in the Gradgrind schoolroom.

29. For one outstanding treatment of this question, see Wayne C. Booth, *The Company We Keep: An Ethics of Fiction* (Berkeley and Los Angeles: University of California Press, 1988).

30. Notice that one of the horrible features of Coketown, from the novel's point of view, is its attempt to erase qualitative distinctions: "It contained several large streets all very like one another, and many small streets still more like one another"; its people are made "to do the same work, and . . . every day was the same as yesterday and tomorrow, and every year the counterpart of the last and next" (65).

31. See the excellent discussion by David Craig in the introduction to Penguin edition.

32. See George Orwell, "Charles Dickens," in Orwell, *Dickens, Dali, and Others* (New York: Harcourt Brace Jovanovich, 1946), 1–75.

33. See a related discussion of this point in Lionel Trilling, "The Princess Casamassima," in *The Liberal Imagination: Essays on Literature and Society* (New York: Charles Scribner's Sons, 1950), and in my "Perception and Revolution," in *Love's Knowledge;* see also chapter 3 for further discussion of this point.

34. This does not mean that there could never be an inegalitarian novel; it does mean that inegalitarianism is in a degree of tension with the structure of the genre, which invites concern and respect for any story to which it directs the reader's attention. The problem, in the case of a novelist such as Proust, will be in the narrow circle of human beings to whose lives our attention is directed. See also Ian Watt, *The Rise of the Novel* (Berkeley and Los Angeles: University of California Press, 1957) and Charles Taylor, *Sources of the Self: The Making of Modern Identity* (Cambridge: Harvard University Press, 1989). There is much to be said in this connection about tensions within the work of a novelist such as D. H. Lawrence, or Henry James, whose *The Princess Casamassima* shows, I believe, that he was a perfectionist rather than an elitist—that he supported the provision of a humanistic and artistic education to all citizens. (See "Perception and Revolution," in *Love's Knowledge.*)

35. See also the passage where Mr. Gradgrind proves that "the Good Samaritan was a Bad Economist" (238).

36. In these ways, the novel constructs, in its imagined reader, an ideal moral judge who bears a close resemblance to the parties in John Rawls's Original Position (*A Theory of Justice*). But the faculties the reader is invited to use would not correspond to Rawls's account of "Considered judgment"—on this see my argument in "Perceptive Equilibrium," in *Love's Knowledge.*

37. Thus the novel embodies a (rather Aristotelian) conception of pleasure according to which pleasure itself contains qualitative distinctions and supervenes on activities of various sorts. Classical utilitarians claim to be maximizing plea-

sure. Why, then, is novel-reading so opposed by Mr. Gradgrind? Apparently the source of opposition is his fear that this reading will cause people to behave in various nonefficient ways in the rest of their lives; thus, from his point of view, it will do more harm than good.

38. See p. 240, where Louisa contrasts the perception of "the shapes and surfaces of things" with the exercise of fancy.

39. On this, see Richard Wollheim, "Seeing-In and Seeing-As," in *Art and Its Objects*, 2d ed. (Cambridge: Harvard University Press, 1980), and *Painting as Art* (Princeton: Princeton University Press, 1987), chap. 2.

40. See the wonderful account in Cavell, *The Claim of Reason*: Wittgenstein, Skepticism, Morality, and Tragedy (New York: Charles Scribner's Sons, 1979), part 4.

41. Thus the circus people are said to be "deserving" of both "respect" and "generous construction" (77); see also Sleary's famous injunction to "make the betht of uth: not the wurtht!" (83).

42. It is part of the novel's claim that the simple economic model does not reliably predict how people will behave: its formulae are not even in that sense useful. See Sen, "Rational Fools."

43. One might compare the account of Emile's education for "pity" or compassion in book 4 of Rousseau's *Emile*, where Emile must learn to have compassion for the sufferings of small animals before he goes on to human beings.

44. See "Steerforth's Arm," in *Love's Knowledge*, where I discuss the way in which his storytelling persona is repeatedly imagined by David Copperfield as feminine. This of course does not imply that Dickens is altogether free of contradiction on this point, as the harsh treatment of Emily shows. In many respects, Dickens appears to be more comfortable endorsing a receptive, playful sexuality in males than in females. But in this novel it is noteworthy that the representative of the artistic imagination, Sissy Jupe, is also the only character to achieve a happy and loving marriage.

45. One might naturally ask, but can't one use fancy to hate? I shall say more about this in chapter 3, where I talk about the range of sentiments the reader is and is not invited, by the novel's form, to have; I connect this with Adam Smith's account of ideal emotional spectatorship. *Hard Times* urges us, further, to consider the nonjudgmental participation of the novel in each and every life, its recognition that each life does have its own story, its invitation to see each life from the person's own point of view. Here, I think, we see what Dickens means by "the great Charity in the heart": the novel, while permitting and even suggesting certain criticisms of its characters, promotes mercy through its invitation to empathetic understanding. Most social hatred involves the refusal to enter into the life of another in thought, to recognize the other as an individual human being

with a distinctive story to tell, someone who one might oneself be. In that sense, the novel cultivates a moral ability that is opposed to hatred in its very structure.

46. Compare Mr. Gradgrind when he is able to see a fire in Louisa's eyes and begins to use metaphorical speech.

47. For more on this, see my "Aristotelian Social Democracy," in *Liberalism and the Good*, ed. R. Bruce Douglass, Gerald M. Mara, and Henry S. Richardson (New York: Routledge, 1990), 203–52; "Aristotle on Human Nature and the Foundations of Ethics," in *World, Mind, and Ethics: Essays on the Philosophy of Bernard Williams*, ed. Ross Harrison and J. E. G. Altham (Cambridge: Cambridge University Press, 1995), 86–131; and "Human Functioning and Social Justice: In Defense of Aristotelian Essentialism," *Political Theory* 20 (1992) 202–46.

48. See here my discussion of the predictions in Posner's *Sex and Reason*, in " 'Only Grey Matter?' Richard Posner's Cost-Benefit Analysis of Sex," *University of Chicago Law Review* 59 (1992): 1689–1734; for critical discussion of the predictive dimension of Philpson and Posner's *Private Choices and Public Health*, see David Charney, "Economics of Death," *Harvard Law Review* 107 (1994): 2056–80. Posner himself states that his account does not correctly predict the decision of the U.S. Supreme Court in the privacy cases (*Economics of Justice*), but he concludes that this is because their choices are not rational in the normative sense. For related criticism of Becker on the family, see Sen, "Gender and Cooperative Conflicts."

49. See Hilary Putnam on the "Super-Benthamites," in *Reason, Truth, and History* (Cambridge: Cambridge University Press, 1982), and the discussion of that passage in Margaret Jane Radin, "Market-Inalienability."

50. Stigler, Convocation Address (see note 15 above).

51. See Amartya Sen, "Internal Consistency of Choice," *Econometrica* 61 (1993): 495 ff. Sen shows that because of the influence of context on choice, choices do not obey even weak axioms of rationality, such as transitivity. (Transitivity says that if A is preferred to B and B to C, then A will be preferred to C.) What these failures show is that we cannot rank-order individual preferences simply on the basis of choices without an account of the evaluations that lie beneath choices.

52. Posner, *The Economics of Justice*, 231 ff.

53. See the excellent statement of this argument in Richardson, *Practical Reasoning*, chap. 5, sec. 15.

54. See Martha Nussbaum and Amartya Sen, eds., *The Quality of Life* (Oxford: Clarendon Press, 1993).

55. To some extent and in some contexts, inroads have been made by other approaches in terms of "basic needs" or, in Sen's approach, in terms of functioning and capability: see United Nations Development Program, *Human Development*

Report 1993 (New York, 1993). On the other hand, the other approach still predominates: see Sen's and my introduction to *The Quality of Life*, and Sen, *Resources, Values, and Development* (Oxford: Basil Blackwell, 1984).

56. See Sen, *Choice, Welfare, and Measurement* and *The Standard of Living*.

57. See Leavis's account of this passage in *The Great Tradition*.

58. For accounts of the approach, see Nussbaum and Sen, *The Quality of Life*, the various writings of Sen cited above, and my articles cited in note 47 above. The implications of the approach for the assessment of women's quality of life are elaborated in Nussbaum and Glover, *Women, Culture, and Development*.

59. See Sen, *Choice, Welfare, and Measurement, The Standard of Living*, and "Capabilities and Well-Being," in Nussbaum and Sen, *The Quality of Life*.

60. See the papers by Robert Erikson and Erik Allardt in Nussbaum and Sen, *The Quality of Life*.

3. Rational Emotions

1. Richard Posner, *The Economics of Justice* (Cambridge: Harvard University Press, 1981), 1–2.

2. The instruction is assessed in *California v. Brown*, 479 U.S. (1986), 538 ff.

3. Ibid., Justice Brennan, dissenting, 554–55. The majority held that the instruction was constitutional because it would be understood by any reasonable juror to mandate the exclusion only of "untethered" or "inappropriate" sympathy; Brennan argues effectively that this has not been the case. All the justices agree that certain types of emotion are in fact legitimate as guides to a rational decision about sentencing.

4. On the emotion-reason distinction in the law, see Paul Gewirtz, "Aeschylus' Law," *Harvard Law Review* 101 (1988): 1043–55; Lynne Henderson, "Legality and Empathy," *Michigan Law Review* 85 (1987): 1574–1652; Toni Massaro, "Empathy, Legal Storytelling, and the Rule of Law: New Words, Old Wounds," *Michigan Law Review* 85 (1989): 2099–2127; and Martha Minow and Elizabeth V. Spelman, "Passion for Justice," *Cardozo Law Review* 10 (1988): 37–76, commenting on Justice Brennan's paper in the same issue. Only Minow and Spelman question the sharp dichotomy between reason and emotion, and none of the articles investigates the role of belief and judgment in the emotions themselves.

5. I state the Stoic view in its full form, and it is a rather extreme view; as we shall see below, one may accept their claim in a modified form, as true of some instances of emoting, without getting rid of emotions completely.

6. On the different positions in the tradition regarding the relationship between belief and emotion, see note 9, below.

7. Irving Howe, *Politics and the Novel* (New York: Horizon Press, 1957). The chapter on James is reprinted in *Henry James: A Collection of Critical Essays*, ed. Leon Edel (Englewood Cliffs, N.J.: Prentice-Hall, 1963), 156–71.

8. For an attempt to do this, see my *Upheavals of Thought: A Theory of the Emotions*, the Gifford Lectures for 1993 (Cambridge: Cambridge University Press, forthcoming 1997).

9. In psychology, see, for example, Richard Lazarus, *Emotion and Adaptation* (Oxford: Oxford University Press, 1991), and A. Ortony, G. Clore, and G. Collins, *The Cognitive Structure of Emotion* (Cambridge: Cambridge University Press, 1991); in anthropology, Jean Briggs, Never in Anger (Cambridge: Harvard University Press, 1981), and Catherine Lutz, *Unnatural Emotions* (Chicago: University of Chicago Press, 1988). The lack of support among philosophers would not be significant in and of itself, since philosophers have been known to agree about wrong conclusions over a long period of time; I mean, however, to focus on the fact that no good *arguments* have been produced to support the point.

10. The Stoics trace their position to Plato (whether rightly or wrongly), and Spinoza and Smith base theirs on that of the Stoics.

11. I defend it in *The Therapy of Desire: Theory and Practice in Hellenistic Ethics* (Princeton: Princeton University Press, 1994), chap. 10, and also in *Upheavals of Thought*.

12. See Kahan and Nussbaum, "Two Conceptions of Emotion in Criminal Law" (manuscript).

13. I use both words because "pity," in recent times, has acquired connotations of condescension that it did not have earlier, and still does not have when used as a translation of Greek *eleos*, Latin *misericordia*, or Rousseau's *pitié*.

14. Consider Gradgrind's appeals to Bitzer to have gratitude for his education and sympathy for Gradgrind's predicament:

> "I really wonder, sir," rejoined the old pupil in an argumentative manner, "to find you taking a position so untenable. My schooling was paid for; it was a bargain; and when I came away, the bargain ended."
>
> It was a fundamental principle of the Gradgrind philosophy, that everything was to be paid for. Nobody was ever on any account to give anybody anything, or render anybody help without purchase. Gratitude was to be abolished, and the virtues springing from it were not to be. Every inch of the existence of mankind, from birth to death, was to be a bargain across a counter. And if we didn't get to Heaven that way, it was not a politico-economical place, and we had no business there.

15. It is plausible only if we carefully bear in mind that the relevant beliefs include evaluations of the importance of the object for the person experiencing the emotion. Two people may judge that "Socrates is dead." If only one also judges,

"Socrates is one of the most important people in the world to me," then only that one will experience grief; but for that one, the belief-set will be sufficient for grief. See my *Upheavals of Thought.*

16. For valuable critiques along these lines, see James Rachels, *Created from Animals* (New York: Oxford University Press, 1990), Jonathan Glover, *Causing Death and Saving Lives* (Harmondsworth: Pelican, 1976); and Richard Posner, *Sex and Reason* (Cambridge: Harvard University Press, 1992).

17. Indeed, we might say that Louisa is attracted to Harthouse precisely because her attachment-world has previously been so empty and uncultivated: she knows how to embrace only the emptiness she feels.

18. Lionel Trilling, *The Liberal Imagination: Essays on Literature and Society* (New York: Charles Scribner's Sons, 1950).

19. Lukács calls *The Home and the World* (which is intensely critical of the early Indian nationalist movement) "a petit bourgeois yarn of the shoddiest kind" (quoted in Anita Desai's introduction to the 1985 Penguin edition of the novel, p. 7). For the case of *The Princess Casamassima*, see Trilling, *The Liberal Imagination*, and my discussion in "Perception and Revolution" in *Love's Knowledge: Essays on Philosophy and Literature:* (New York: Oxford University Press, 1990).

20. As the impoverished trader Panchu says to Nikhil, "I am afraid, sir, . . . while you big folk are doing the fighting, the police and the law vultures will merrily gather round, and the crowd will enjoy the fun, but when it comes to getting killed, it will be the turn of only poor me." We see the commitments of the genre, as well, in Nikhil's refusal to dismiss the English governess: "I cannot . . . look upon Miss Gilby through a mist of abstraction, just because she is English. Cannot you get over the barrier of her name after such a long acquaintance? Cannot you realize that she loves you?" This is a self-referential moment: for it is evident that the vision of the novel as a whole is this sort of particularized vision.

21. Raymond Williams, *The Politics of Modernism: Against the New Conformists* (London and New York: Verso, 1989), 116.

22. Williams would certainly agree: see his valuable account of the novel in *Culture and Society, 1780–1950* (London: Penguin, 1958), part 1, chap. 5.

23. This device, in which circumstantial and informational restrictions are used to model the moral point of view, was in many respects the origin of John Rawls's device of the Original Position in *A Theory of Justice* (Cambridge: Harvard University Press, 1971).

24. Smith would include the love we have for friends and fellow citizens, as well as the love of humanity; he excludes only erotic love, which he takes to be based on morally irrelevant particularities and to be inexplicable by any kind of public reason-giving process.

25. On the need for reflective criticism, see also the title essay in *Love's Knowledge*.

26. *California v. Brown*, 538.

27. *Woodson v. North Carolina*, 428 U.S. 280, 304 (1976).

4. Poets as Judges

1. *Nicomachean Ethics* 5. 1137b27–32.

2. For related accounts of nondeductive practical judgment, see Charles Taylor, *Sources of the Self: The Making of Modern Identity* (Cambridge: Harvard University Press, 1989); and with respect to literary readership, Wayne C. Booth, *The Company We Keep: An Ethics of Fiction* (Berkeley and Los Angeles: University of California Press, 1988). On Aristotle's similar view, see my essay "The Discernment of Perception," in *Love's Knowledge: Essays on Philosophy and Literature*.

3. Stanley Fish, especially *Doing What Comes Naturally* (Durham: Duke University Press, 1989), and *There's No Such Thing as Free Speech and It's a Good Thing Too* (Cambridge: Harvard University Press, 1993).

4. See my "Skepticism about Practical Reason in Literature and the Law," *Harvard Law Review* 107 (1994): 714–44. Fish does not accept the label "skeptic," since he holds that we are caused by our traditions and our psychology to have and act on certain definite beliefs, and in that sense we are not free to play or even to question. I argue that this was, in fact, exactly the view of the ancient Greek skeptics, and their solution to the question of how and why the skeptic would act. Once we give up on good reasons for action, we are left with causes of action that may move us with necessitating force.

5. Benjamin Cardozo, *The Nature of the Judicial Process* (New York, 1921), 166–67.

6. Christopher Columbus Langdell, speech of 1887, quoted in William Twining, *Karl Llewelyn and the Realist Movement* (Norman: University of Oklahoma Press, 1985), 11.

7. For further discussion of this, see my "The Discernment of Perception," in *Love's Knowledge*, and "Equity and Mercy," *Philosophy and Public Affairs* 22 (1993): 83–125. For an excellent discussion of these issues in the law, see Cass Sunstein, *Political Conflict and the Rule of Law* (New York: Oxford University Press, forthcoming).

8. Herbert Wechsler, "Toward Neutral Principles of Constitutional Law," *Harvard Law Review* 73 (1959).

9. See Raoul Hilberg, *The Destruction of the European Jews*, student edition (New York: Holmes and Meier, 1985).

10. Richard Wright, *Native Son* (New York: Harper, 1993), 1. All quotes are from this unexpurgated edition of the novel.

11. See my "Equity and Mercy," reprinted in *Punishment*, A. John Simmons et al. (Princeton: Princeton University Press, 1994), 145–87.

12. E. M. Forster, "Terminal Note" to *Maurice* (New York: W. W. Norton, 1971), 250. All page numbers are from this paperback edition.

13. *Hudson v. Palmer*, 468 U.S. 517, 82 L. Ed. 2d 393, 104 S. Ct. 3194 (1984), 393 ff.

14. The officers found a ripped pillowcase in the waste basket and as a result brought charges against Palmer for destroying state property; he was ordered to reimburse the state, and a reprimand was entered on his record.

15. In a curious sentence at the beginning of this section, Stevens uses the name "Hudson" where he should have said "Palmer": "Even if it is assumed that Hudson had no reasonable expectation of privacy in most of the property at issue . . ." (413). The literary judge should not confuse one character with another, but perhaps this was some sort of error in transcription!

16. Stevens adds arguments deriving from the Eighth and the First Amendments, which I shall not consider here.

17. Richard Posner, *The Economics of Justice* (Cambridge: Harvard University Press, 1981).

18. Richard Posner, *Sex and Reason* (Cambridge: Harvard University Press, 1992), and "The Economic Approach to Homosexuality," in *Laws and Nature: Shaping Sex, Preference, and Family* ed. David Estlund and Martha Nussbaum, (Oxford: Oxford University Press, forthcoming 1996).

19. *Mary Jane Carr v. Allison Gas Turbine Division, General Motors Corporation*, 32 F. 3d 1007 (7th Cir. 1994).

20. A large proportion of judicial opinions are written by law clerks, and citations are especially likely to be chosen by clerks.

21. *Bowers v. Hardwick*, 478 U.S. 186 (1986).

22. A peculiarity of the situation discussed by Posner in his excellent treatment of the case (*Sex and Reason*, 341–50) was that in common law, sodomy did not include fellatio but was limited to anal intercourse; the extension took place late in the nineteenth century. On the heterosexual issue, the plaintiffs at one point introduced a motion asking that all members of the Georgia prosecutor's office who had ever committed sodomy disqualify themselves; the motion was denied.

23. See Posner, *Sex and Reason*, 342: "Had he noted that besides being about family, marriage, and procreation, [these] cases had been about sex, he could not have polished them off so easily." Also Thomas Grey, "Eros, Civilization, and the Burger Court," *Law and Contemporary Problems* 43 (1980): 83 ff.

24. For another example of Justice White's distancing tactic, see Richard Posner, *Law and Literature: A Misunderstood Relation* (Cambridge: Harvard University Press, 1988), 308–9, discussing the statement of facts in *Cox Broadcasting Corp. v. Cohn*, 420 U.S. 469, 471 (1975), a case holding that a state may not allow the family of a rape victim, killed by the rapists, to get damages for the invasion of privacy caused by broadcasting the victim's name. White begins: "In August 1971, ap-

pellee's 17-year-old daughter was the victim of a rape and did not survive the incident." As Posner points out, the Court "shied away from stating the blunt truth" (that the victim was murdered).

25. *Kelley v. Johnson*, 425 U.S. 238 (1976).

26. On the Greek world, see K. J. Dover, *Greek Homosexuality*, 2d ed. (Cambridge: Harvard University Press, 1986); for connections to the contemporary issues, see Dover's autobiography, *Marginal Comment* (London: Duckworth, 1994). See also my "Platonic Love and Colorado Law: The Relevance of Ancient Greek Norms to Modern Sexual Controversies," *Virginia Law Review* 80 (1994) 601– 738; (appendix 4 is coauthored by me and Kenneth Dover). On Christian traditions, see, among other works, John Boswell, *Christianity, Social Tolerance, and Homosexuality* (Chicago: University of Chicago Press, 1980); for a detailed argument concerning interpretation of the relevant passages from Leviticus, see Saul Olyan, "And with a Man You Shall Not Lie the Lying Down of a Woman," *Journal of the History of Sexuality* 5 (1974): 179ff.

27. The issues on both sides, in four leading American religious traditions, were presented at a conference at Brown University, April 7–8, 1995, and will be published in a book to be edited by Saul Olyan and me. For one impressive example of recent rethinking of traditional norms, see the statements by theologians and various groups within the Norwegian Lutheran Church collected in the preamble to the recent domestic-partner legislation for same-sex couples passed by the Norwegian parliament in 1993.

28. Cass Sunstein, "Sexual Orientation and the Constitution: A Note on the Relationship between Due Process and Equal Protection," *University of Chicago Law Review* 55 (1988): 1161ff. Equal protection arguments have been used in lower court gay-rights cases, although so far all decisions using such arguments have been overturned.

29. See Posner, *Sex and Reason*.

[Index]